THE TOTAL ROCK GUITARIST

>> A Fun and Comprehensive Overview of Rock Guitar Playing

TOBIAS HURWITZ

Alfred, the leader in educational publishing,

and the National Guitar Workshop,

one of America's finest guitar schools, have joined

forces to bring you the best, most progressive

educational tools possible. We hope you will enjoy

this book and encourage you to look for

other fine products from Alfred and the

National Guitar Workshop.

Alfred Publishing Co., Inc.
16320 Roscoe Blvd., Suite 100
P.O. Box 10003
Van Nuys, CA 91410-0003
alfred.com

ISBN-10: 0-7390-3850-8 (Book & CD)
ISBN-13: 978-0-7390-3850-5 (Book & CD)

This book was acquired, edited and produced
by Workshop Arts, Inc., the publishing arm of
the National Guitar Workshop.
Nathaniel Gunod, acquisitions, managing editor
Burgess Speed, editor
Matthew Liston, assistant editor
Timothy Phelps, interior design & photography
Ante Gelo, music typesetter
CD recorded by Mark Schane-Lydon at WorkshopLive.com, Pittsfield, MA

Cover guitar courtesy of Fender Musical Instruments
Cover photograph: Dynamic Graphics Group/Creatas/Almay

Table of Contents

About the Author

GIT graduate **Tobias Hurwitz** resides in Baltimore, Maryland, where he has been playing rock guitar since 1977. You can hear him on his two instrumental releases, *Painted Sky,* which features P-Funk alumnus Dennis Chambers on drums, and *The Way of Zen Guitar,* which is a tribute to the music and philosophy of Philip Toshio Sudo.

Tobias has been published in *Guitar Player, Guitar One* and *Guitar*, and has authored many books for Alfred/National Guitar Workshop (see list below). He has jammed or recorded with many musical giants including J. Geils, Stanley Clarke, Michael Angelo Batio and The Coasters. Tobias is deeply involved in the Zen Guitar movement sparked by the book *Zen Guitar,* by Philip Toshio Sudo.

Tobias gives solo guitar clinics and performs with his own band in the Mid-Atlantic region. You can study guitar with Tobias online at WorkshopLive.com. He endorses PRS Guitars, Ernie Ball Strings and Budda Amplification.

For more on Tobias visit:
www.tobiashurwitz.com   www.shredplanet.com
www.zenguitar.com   www.workshoplive.com

PHOTO BY J. VICTOR ELLIOT

Other Publications by Tobias Hurwitz:
Play Rock Guitar: Getting Started (National Guitar Workshop #07-1101)
Rock Chops for Guitar (National Guitar Workshop #07-1039)
Guitar Shop: Getting Your Sound (Alfred/National Guitar Workshop #18424)
Guitar Styles: Punk Rock (Alfred/NGW #18509)
Guitar Technique Encyclopedia (with various authors; Alfred/NGW #19381)
Learn How to Transcribe for Guitar (Alfred/NGW #14948)
7-String Guitar (with Glenn Riley; Alfred/NGW #21892)

Acknowledgements

Special thanks to: My lovely and talented girlfriend, Terry Gourley, and her two cats, Joey and Sophie, for making our house a home (the Lilith Licks are dedicated to you, Terry); my family: Francis, Jerry, Toby and Gandhi.

Winn Krozack, PRS Guitars, the crews of Ernie Ball Strings, *Guitar Player* magazine, ZenGuitar.com, and ShredPlanet.com, Burgess Speed, Billyjack Mast, Voodoo Blue, Dave Smolover, Nat Gunod, Paula Abate, Steve Wnuk, and the crews of Workshop Arts Publications, the National Guitar Workshop, DayJams and WorkshopLive.

My original guitar mentors: Ric Rutledge and Sifu John Thompson, and a more recent mentor, Philip Toshio Sudo—may his vision live on.

Introduction

The Total Rock Guitarist is a complete rock guitar method that covers the bases from the beginning level to advanced. The CD includes recordings of the most important examples, and backing tracks to jam along with.

This book has everything you need. It is a reference book filled with chords, scales, techniques, etudes and examples, and flows smoothly from beginning to intermediate to advanced in the realms of rhythm guitar, lead guitar and theory. There's also a Getting Started (page 6) section that explains how to stretch, warm up, tune and correctly position both of your hands.

So whether you're using this as a reference book, a page-by-page method book or just a cool riff book, I hope you dig in hard and glean some of the knowledge I've gathered over the last 30 years of playing rock guitar.

Punky Meadows of the band Angel once encouraged me to "stay on the neck." I took his advice to heart, and now I pass it on to you. We all know that the only way to become a great rock guitarist is to love the music and play a whole lot! I hope this book provides you with the materials, insight and inspiration to achieve your goals. Enjoy!

Tobias Hurwitz

A Word on Music Notation and Theory

Knowing how to read music written in standard notation and TAB will help you to get the most from The Total Rock Guitarist. If you don't know how to read music, you may wish to skip ahead to the Appendix (page 112) and Reading Music (page 124) for a quick introduction.

The Appendix covers many important concepts including scale construction, key signatures, chord formulas, tetrachords and inversions. While you don't need to understand these concepts to play the examples in this book, learning them will make you a more well-rounded musician and help you to write your own songs, licks and riffs.

0
Track 0.0

A compact disc is available with this book. Using the disc will help make learning more enjoyable and the information more meaningful. Listening to the CD will help you correctly interpret the rhythms and feel of each example. The symbol at the upper left appears next to each song or example that is performed on the CD. Example numbers are above the symbol. The track number below each symbol corresponds directly to the song or example you want to hear. In most cases, there is more than one example per track; this is reflected in the track numbers (for example: track 2.1, track 2.2, track 2.3, etc.).

Track 1 will help you tune to this CD.

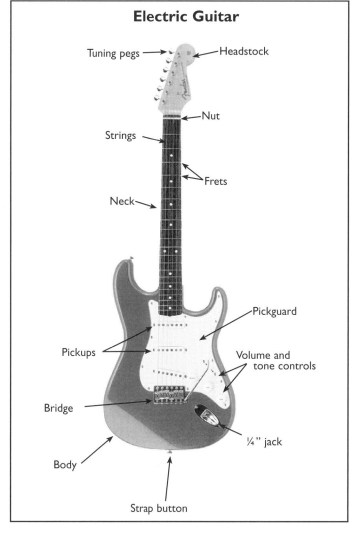

Electric Guitar

Tuning pegs
Headstock
Nut
Strings
Frets
Neck
Pickguard
Pickups
Volume and tone controls
Bridge
¼" jack
Body
Strap button

PART 1: Getting Started

Holding the Guitar

Let's get started by learning how to properly hold the guitar.

This picture shows a good sitting position.

This picture shows a good standing position.

Good sitting position.

Good standing position.

Notice how the guitar stays at the same level when sitting or standing. Adjust your strap so that your guitar does not become awkwardly higher or lower when you stand up. Playing with a low-strung strap might look cool, but it makes playing more difficult.

Thumb Position

To the right is an example of good thumb position. Holding your thumb in this position will help keep your wrist straight. At times, you can wrap your thumb around the top of the neck, like Jimi Hendrix often did, to fret the bass string with your thumb.

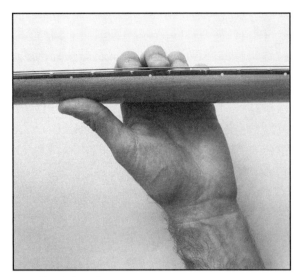

Good thumb position.

To the right is an example of bad thumb position. Holding the thumb in this position causes the wrist to be awkwardly bent.

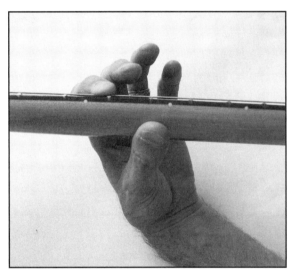

Bad thumb position.

Wrist Position

Thumb position affects wrist position, which is a key element of good technique in *both* hands. Keep your wrists as straight as possible while playing guitar (see photo demonstrating good thumb position at the top of this page). This facilitates ease of motion and decreases the chance of injury. It is a challenge to keep both wrists straight and also maintain good thumb position in all playing situations, so just do your best. The more years you play guitar, the more limber you will become, and the better your playing posture will be.

Picking Grip

The picture below shows the best picking grip. This grip is used for everything except strumming fast, which requires a loose wrist.

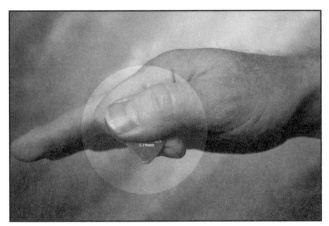

Picking grip.

Strumming Grip

The picture below shows the best strumming grip. It is only a slight variation on the picking grip and is used for fast strumming.

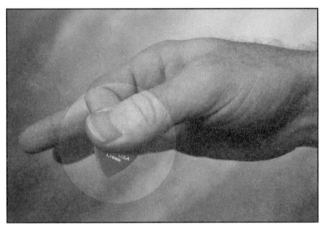

Strumming grip.

Notice that both grips are between the thumb and 1st finger. It's important to use only these two fingers, and not the ring finger, for these reasons:

- To facilitate *hybrid picking* (where the other three fingers are used to pick or finger tap additional strings).
- To maintain the straightest possible wrist.

Stretching and Warming Up

Rock guitar playing often gives the hands and arms an intensive workout, so, we guitarists should all get into the habit of stretching and warming up before practicing or playing a gig. This can help ward off annoying hand disorders like tendonitis and carpal tunnel syndrome. Be careful not to injure yourself by stretching too hard.

Stretching

Stretch No. 1

Place your palms together with the fingers pointed up as if praying. Lower your hands while keeping the palms together. You should feel the stretch in both wrists.

Stretch No. 1.

Stretch No. 2

While in the same position as stretch 1, tilt your hands forward, so that the fingers point straight ahead, or slightly down. You should feel the stretch moving up your forearms.

Stretch No. 2.

Stretch No. 3

Raise both arms straight in front of you with your elbows bent so that the backs of your wrists touch each other and your fingers are pointed down. Rotate your hands as fully as possible while keeping the backs of the wrists together. You should feel the stretch in the joints of both wrists.

Stretch No. 3.

Stretch No. 4

Bend each individual finger back with the palm of the opposite hand. Do this with both hands, so that all ten fingers are stretched.

Stretch No. 4.

Warming Up

Warming up gets blood flowing to the muscles before playing.

Warm-Up No. 1

Massage each finger by rubbing and pulling it with the thumb and fingers of the opposite hand. Do this to all ten fingers.

Warm-Up No. 2

Play any exercise or passage very slowly, so that there is no hand stress involved.

Paying attention to good playing posture and remembering to stretch and warm up is really important, and the benefits will be well worth the effort.

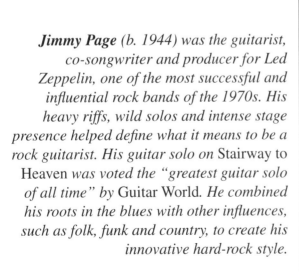

Jimmy Page (b. 1944) was the guitarist, co-songwriter and producer for Led Zeppelin, one of the most successful and influential rock bands of the 1970s. His heavy riffs, wild solos and intense stage presence helped define what it means to be a rock guitarist. His guitar solo on Stairway to Heaven *was voted the "greatest guitar solo of all time" by* Guitar World. *He combined his roots in the blues with other influences, such as folk, funk and country, to create his innovative hard-rock style.*

Tuning Up

Tuning your guitar is an important step on the road to sounding great. In this section we're going to talk about three popular tuning methods and some unique aspects of guitar tuning. (You can also tune to track 1 of the CD.)

Tuning your guitar properly requires a good understanding of *pitch*. In scientific terms, pitch refers to the exact *frequency* (cycles per second) of a tone. In practical terms, pitch refers to the note name you are playing (C, B$\flat$, F$\sharp$, etc.) and whether it is *sharp* (too high), *flat* (too low) or perfectly in tune. In other words, pitch refers to the highness or lowness of a tone.

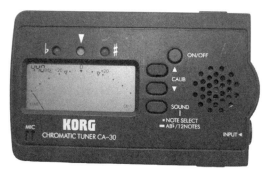

Electronic tuner.

Using an Electronic Tuner

An *electronic tuner* (also called a *digital tuner*) is an inexpensive device available at any music store. *Guitar tuners* sense only the pitches of standard guitar tuning (E, A, D, G, B and E). *Chromatic tuners* can be used to tune to any pitch, so they are useful if you play other instruments or use non-standard guitar tunings.

First, plug your guitar into the input of the tuner, turn the tuner on, and make sure that the volume is fully up on your guitar. The idea is to turn the tuning peg on your guitar until the needle points to the middle; this indicates that the string is properly tuned.

Some tuners require you to select each string for tuning, but most will automatically "sense" the string. This can sometimes be tricky; if you are tuning the D string, and it is so high that it is closer to the note E than to D, you may end up tuning your D string to the pitch of E. So, you must be sure you're on the correct string. Electronic tuners work much better for "fine tuning" than for tuning a guitar that is really far off. Also it helps to be an experienced guitarist, so you can tell if the string tension is "in the ballpark" just by feel.

You'll notice that when you pluck a note on the guitar, the needle, or LED display, does not register a steady note. It tends to "bounce" up to a high point, then settle briefly at a lower point, then fall off altogether. The harder you pluck the string, the higher the high point gets. This is because the string vibrates more widely the harder you pick it. The more widely it vibrates, the higher the pitch gets. So, you should pick all notes lightly and evenly while tuning. Tune to the point where the note settles, not the high point to which it first bounces. *Harmonics* (see page 82) at the 12th fret work best on most guitar tuners because "string bounce" is greatly minimized with harmonics.

Comparative Tuning

This method involves comparing fretted notes on the 5th and 4th frets to their open-string equivalents. If your low-E string is not tuned to *standard pitch* (the tuning commonly used for electronic tuners, keyboards and Track I of the accompanying CD; also known as *A440*) when you begin, your guitar will end up sounding in tune with *itself*, but not with other instruments or recordings that are tuned to standard pitch.

Step 1) Compare the A on the 5th fret of the low-E string to the open A string. Adjust the A string to match the pitch if necessary.

Step 2) Compare the D on the 5th fret of the A string to the open D string. Adjust if necessary.

Step 3) Compare the G on the 5th fret of the D string to the open G string. Adjust if necessary.

Step 4) Compare the B on the 4th fret of the G string to the open B string. Adjust if necessary.

Step 5) Compare the E on the 5th fret of the B string to the high-E string. Adjust if necessary.

Step 6) Compare both E strings. They should blend perfectly. If they do not blend, adjust the high E to the low E and then work backwards from step five until each note pair matches.

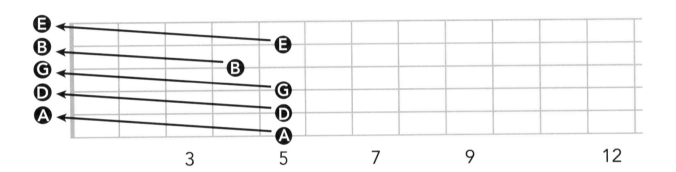

Important tip: Place your left-hand fingertips just to the left of the fret wire. Don't press too hard; this will change the pitch of the note.

Tuning with Harmonics

This method involves comparing *natural harmonics* (notes played by picking a string while gently touching it in exactly the right spot with a left-hand finger; see page 82) on the 5th, 4th and 7th frets. Remember, if your low-E string is not tuned to standard pitch when you begin, your guitar will end up sounding in tune with itself, but not with instruments or recordings that are tuned to standard pitch.

Step 1) Compare the E harmonic on the 5th fret of the low-E string to the E harmonic on the 7th fret of the A string. Adjust the A string to match if necessary.

Step 2) Compare the A harmonic on the 5th fret of the A string to the A harmonic on the 7th fret of the D string. Adjust if necessary.

Step 3) Compare the D harmonic on the 5th fret of the D string to the D harmonic on the 7th fret of the G string. Adjust if necessary.

Step 4) Compare the B harmonic on the 4th fret of the G string to the B harmonic on the 5th fret of the B string. Adjust if necessary.

Step 5) Compare the B harmonic on the 5th fret of the B string to the B harmonic on the 7th fret of the high-E string. Adjust if necessary.

Step 6) Compare the harmonics of both E strings at the 12th fret. They should blend perfectly. If they do not blend, adjust the high E to the low E and then work backwards from Step 5 until each harmonic pair matches.

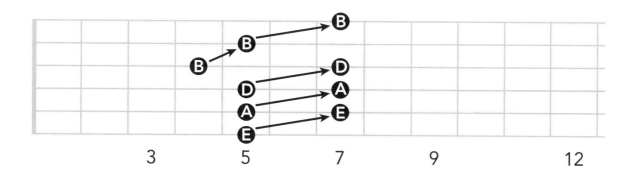

A Word on Tempering

Have you ever noticed that, no matter which tuning method you use, certain chords will tend to ring harmoniously on your guitar, while others will not? This is because the guitar is not a perfect instrument. *Tempering* is the art of evenly distributing tuning problems over the entire playing range of an instrument, so that no one area sounds obviously out of tune.

Standard methods of tempering keyboard instruments have been in place since the Baroque Era (1600–1750). Unfortunately, no such standard methods are in place for tempering guitars. There is only one "official" method available, which is called *The Buzz Feiten Tuning System*. This is an add-on feature requiring modifications to the guitar's nut and bridge.

By checking chords in various positions and *types* (major, minor, etc.) all over the fretboard, you can make slight adjustments that cause all of the chords to ring pleasantly enough on most guitars. Try slightly lowering the high-E and G strings. This is not a standard method, and will vary from guitar to guitar and player to player. The better your ear gets, the more you will notice and be able to handle tuning subtleties.

__Eddie Van Halen__ is well known for his attention to tuning subtleties. He often retunes his guitars from song to song (slightly flatting the B string, for example) to create harmonious chords in a particular key.

PART 2: Chords and Rhythm Guitar

Easy Chords for the Beginner

A *chord* is a group of three or more notes played simultaneously. It is common, however, for guitar players to refer to two-note groupings as chords also. The chords in this chapter are great to start with because they only require one or two fingers to play. Before going any further, you may find it helpful to review page 123 for an explanation of how to read chord diagrams.

Left-Hand Technique

Press your fingertips straight down against the fretboard when you finger a chord so that they don't lean over, accidentally stopping other strings from ringing. You should also press hard enough that the notes sound clear, not fuzzy. This may take some practice and should callous the tips of your fingers eventually. Also, if you place your fingertip right next to the fret, the note will sound better and will be easier to play.

Right-Hand Technique

Make sure you're using one of the correct pick grips from page 8. Rest your pick on the string you intend to start strumming. This string will vary from chord to chord. The pointed tip of the pick should be slightly higher than the larger end that you grip. Strum down across the strings with a gentle, smooth downstroke that is actuated from the elbow and slightly modified by the wrist. This should produce a nicely strummed chord.

Here are some easy one- and two-finger chords for you to try. Be sure to memorize the name of each chord. If you just know the shape, and not the name, you haven't really learned the chord.

Easy Chords

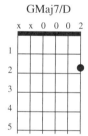
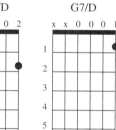

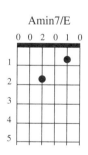
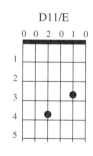

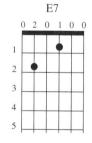

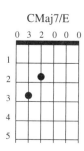
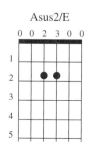

OK, now that you've learned a few easy chords, it's time to begin switching from one chord to another. This is one of the most important skills for any guitarist. Try these exercises. Just strum each chord with a gentle, smooth downstroke ⊓ of your pick, once for each mark above the chord. You may find it useful to review Reading Music (starting on page 124) before trying these exercises.

⊓ = *Downstroke*

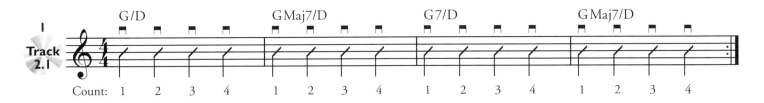

And Now for Some "Real" Chords!

The chords you've been playing so far were designed to be easy. The E7, Emin, Emin7 and D⁶/F♯ appear unmodified— the way they would be strummed in "real" situations—but the others are simplified versions that are not commonly used outside of instructional books.

This next group of chords, though still on the beginning level, are all in their "complete" forms.

"Real" Chords

A 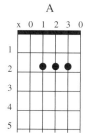	Amin 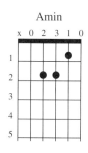	A7 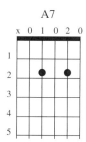	Bmin/F# 
B7 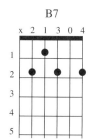	C 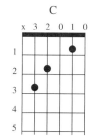	C7 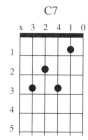	Cadd9 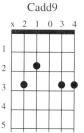
D 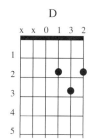	Dmin 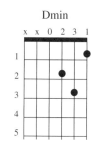	D7 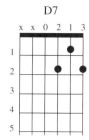	E 

The number in parentheses indicates this is another version of the chord; in this case, the 2nd version.

F 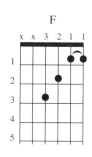	G 	G (2) 	G7 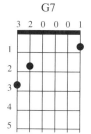

"Real" Chord Progressions

A *progression* is a series of chords. Sometimes, a single progression is used for an entire song. Songs like "What I Got," by Sublime, "Hey Joe," by Jimi Hendrix and "Louie Louie," by The Kingsmen, use one simple chord progression per song. The common rock chord progressions below are great practice material. You should master all of them. First, strum the progression with the simple downstrokes ⊓ indicated above the chords. If you get more ambitious, you can try the more complex strumming involving upstrokes V (Examples 5a, 6a and 7a). Before tackling the more complex patterns, you may find it helpful to review Eighth-Note Strumming Logic (page 22) and Sixteenth-Note Strumming Logic (page 24).

V = Upstroke

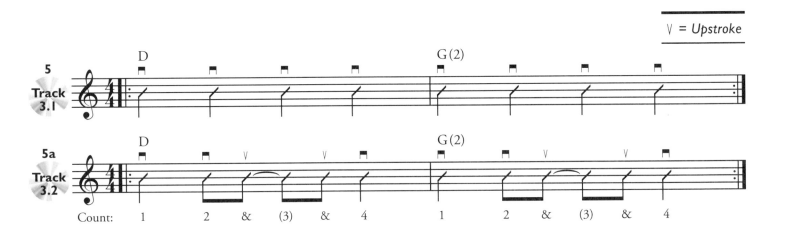

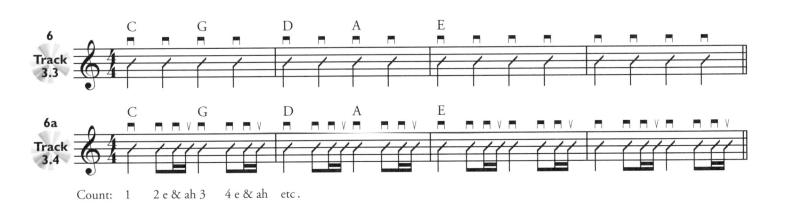

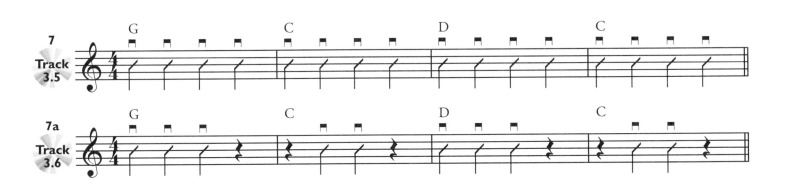

Adding or Subtracting Fingers

Rock music is mainly learned by watching, listening and experimentation. It's a safe bet that Keith Richards didn't hand Mick Jagger the sheet music to "Satisfaction" and ask him if he thought it was OK. He probably just said something like, "Hey man, it goes like this. What do you think?"

The chords below and the exercises that follow (page 20) come from adding or subtracting a finger to or from the chords you already know. In addition to memorizing them and practicing the examples, experiment on your own: Try them on different frets and with different open strings. Arrange them in different sequences. Try a different fingering and check out the sound. Maybe you've just written part of your first song!

Amin7	Amin7 (2)	Asus2	Asus4	A7sus4	AMaj7	Amin add9
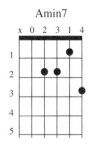	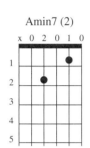		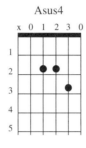	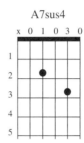	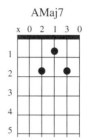	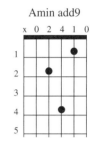

B	CMaj7	Cadd9 (2)	C/G	Dsus2	Dsus4	DMaj7
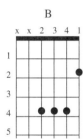	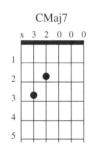		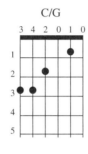		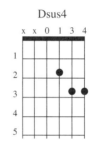	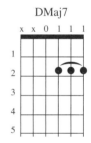

T = Left-hand thumb

Dmin7	D/F♯	D/F♯ (2)	Emin add9	Eadd9	Emin7 (2)	E7 (2)
	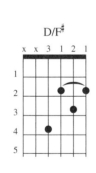	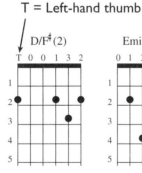	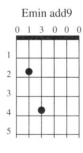			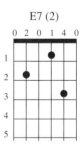

Esus4	E7sus4	FMaj7	GMaj7	EMaj7	G6	Gmin/D
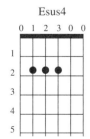	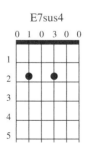		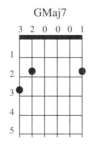	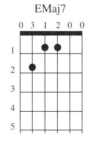	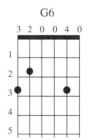	

Examples 8 and 9 make *arpeggios* of your new chords. An *arpeggio* consists of the notes of a chord played separately. Be sure to follow the picking strokes and fingerings. Practice until the chord changes are smooth and the notes are clear.

Note: These examples are the first in the book that use *standard music notation* and TAB. For an explanation of these concepts, see Reading Music on page 124.

About effects: Many of the examples on the CD were recorded with various *digital effects*. For more information on using effects, check out *Guitar Shop: Getting Your Sound* (Alfred/National Guitar Workshop #18424), also by Tobias Hurwitz.

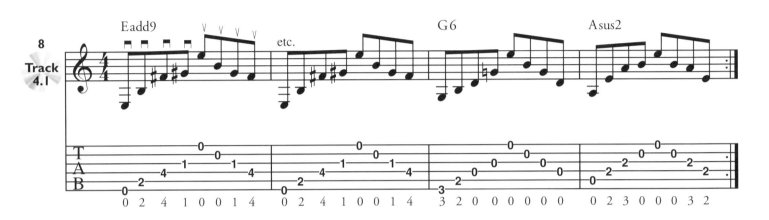

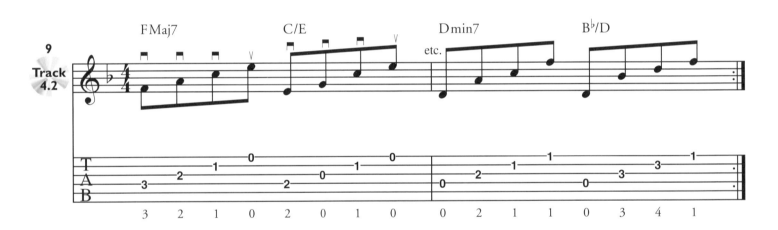

This example adds more new chords and has two strumming styles for you to try. First, try the easy downstroke method using only quarter notes. Then, there is a more complex strumming pattern (Example 10a) that incorporates some upstrokes and *syncopated* (in this case, tied across the beat; see page 23) sixteenth notes.

If you have trouble with the harder strumming, you may wish to revisit it later, after you've been playing a bit longer. You should also simply try strumming with your own natural rhythm.

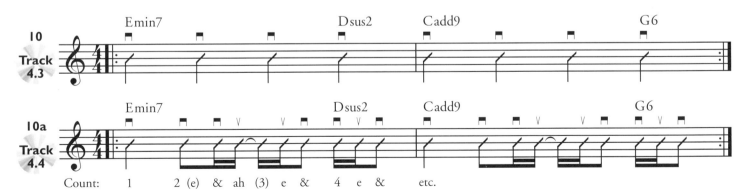

Slash Chords

Slash chords are chords in which the lowest pitched note in the chord is not the *root* (the note that gives the chord its name; see page 115 for more chord theory). If you were to strum the A chord you learned on page 17, its root would be A. If you were to strum it from the 6th string, so that the lowest note was E, then it would become a slash chord, and would be labeled like this: A/E. This chord could also be referred to as *A over E*, meaning an A chord over an E bass note.

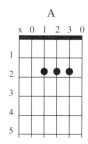 

A few common slash chords are shown below. You should strum each one and listen to how the bass note affects the sound. You have already learned a few others (see pages 15, 17 and 19).

 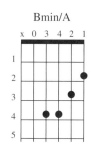 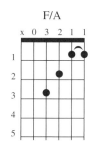 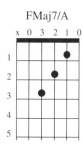 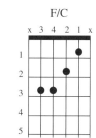

In the chords below, the different bass note can actually change the name of the chord. So, there are two correct names, the slash chord name and the one below it in parentheses.

Eighth-Note Strumming Logic

Strumming logic is knowing when to strum down and up.

Step 1) Tap your foot steadily and count "1, 2, 3, 4, 1, 2, 3, 4," etc., saying each number as your foot comes down.

Understand that you're tapping once per beat and that the kind of notes you're tapping are called quarter notes. This is because they represent one quarter of the common measurement of musical time, which is called a *bar* or a *measure* and commonly lasts for four beats.

Step 2) As you continue tapping and counting, try to imagine that your toe is hitting a little shelf every time your foot comes up. It hits the shelf half way between each tap because your foot must come up before it can come down again. When your foot comes up and hits the shelf, say "and" (&) each time. Now you're counting eighth notes like this:

"1–&, 2–&, 3–&, 4–&," etc.

Your foot is still only tapping on the numbers (the *onbeats*), but you are counting the &'s (the *offbeats*) and the numbers. You can also think of this as "down–up–down–up" etc.

Step 3) Put a guitar pick in your hand and move it down and up as your foot continues to move down and up. The foot goes down, the pick goes down; the foot goes up, the pick goes up. Now start strumming an E chord as you continue to tap your foot. You are strumming down–up–down–up right along with your foot. You are strumming an eighth-note rhythm. There are 8 eighth notes per bar, or two per beat.

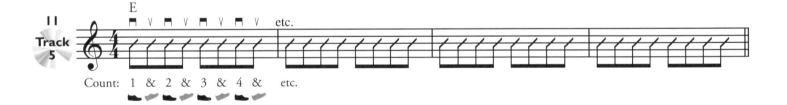

Now we're going to try some exercises in which we strum a combination of quarter notes and eighth notes. The tricky part will be counting steadily as you play and making sure your hand is always strumming down on a number (1, 2, 3, 4) and up on an & ("and"). Just keep your hand swinging steadily down and up, and only attack the strings when the music tells you to.

The strumming becomes more challenging as you move down the page.

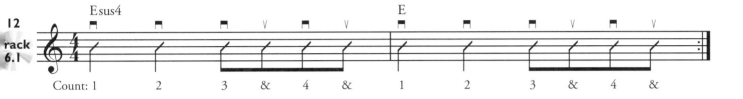

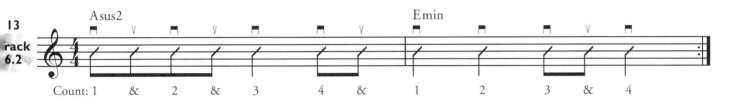

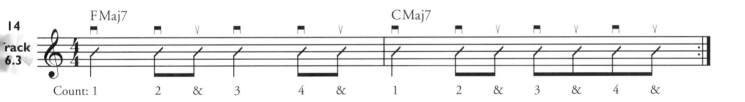

This last example features *syncopation*. In this case, syncopation is the strumming of a normally unaccented beat which then sustains across a normally accented beat. You'll find that the & of beat 2 is strummed and then sustained across beat 3, so that the next strum is on the & of beat 3. That's two upstrokes in a row and is where the syncopation occurs in Example 15. Syncopation can be difficult to master, and may require more practice than the non-syncopated examples.

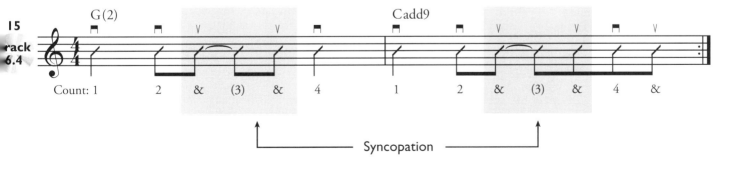

Sixteenth-Note Strumming Logic

There are four sixteenth notes per beat and 16 of them per bar. Sixteenth notes are counted and played like this:

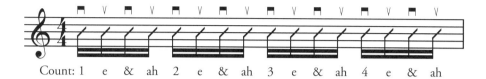

The next set of examples will all be played using sixteenth-note strumming logic.

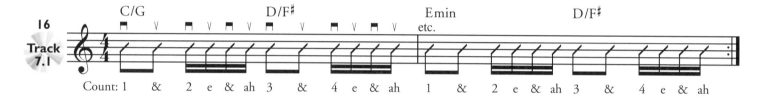

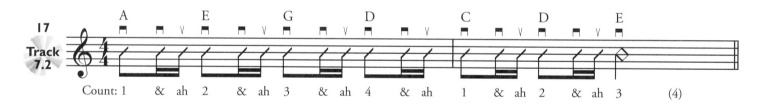

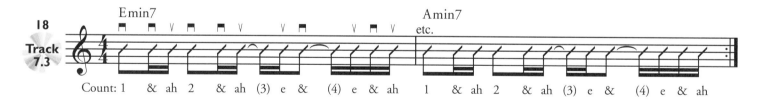

The Blues

The blues is one of rock's biggest influences. Robert Johnson, alone, wrote or heavily influenced songs like "The Lemon Song" by Led Zeppelin, Eric Clapton's version of "Crossroads," The Blues Brothers' version of "Sweet Home Chicago," and The Red Hot Chili Peppers' version of "They're Red Hot." This only scratches the surface of the blues influence without even mentioning the obvious importance of B. B. King, Chuck Berry, Muddy Waters and a host of other blues musicians.

The Standard 12-Bar Blues Form

To understand blues, we must first learn some basic blues *forms*. A form is a chord progression of a particular length, such as 8, 10 or 12 bars, which is used and re-used as the basis for many songs in the same style. We will begin by exploring the standard *12-bar blues form*, which is so popular that it acts as a common ground for musicians of different backgrounds and cultures.

Slash notation, which tells you to strum in any pattern you choose, is used for the example below. For now, however, just strum each chord four times per bar, to get a feel for the progression. Led Zeppelin's "Rock and Roll" and Stevie Ray Vaughan's "Pride and Joy" both use this common form.

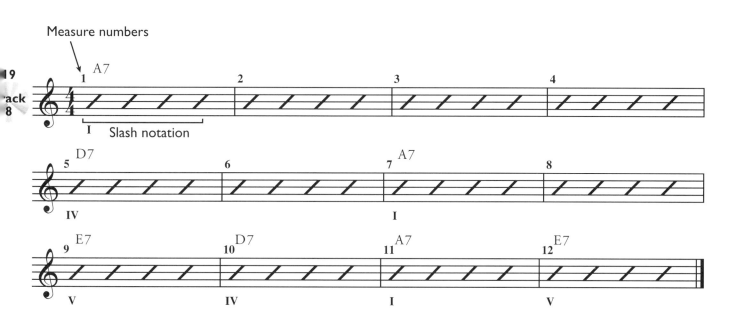

In the example above, the Roman numerals below each chord represent the degree of the corresponding scale upon which the chord is built. This blues is in the key of A, so the names of the notes in an A Major scale are seen below with the corresponding numerals below them. Eventually, knowledge of theory will help you play the blues in any key.

A	B	C♯	D	E	F♯	G♯	A
I	ii	iii	IV	V	vi	vii	I

It's important to study up on this in greater depth by referring to the Introduction to Music Theory section on page 112.

Roman Numeral Review	
I or i 1	V or v 5
II or ii 2	VI or vi 6
III or iii 3	VII or vii 7
IV or iv 4	

Variations on the Standard 12-Bar Blues Form

The Quick Change 12-Bar Blues Form

The *quick change* variation moves to the IV chord in the 2nd measure, then back to the I. Stevie Ray Vaughan's "Love Me Darlin'" and Robert Johnson's "Sweet Home Chicago" both use this form.

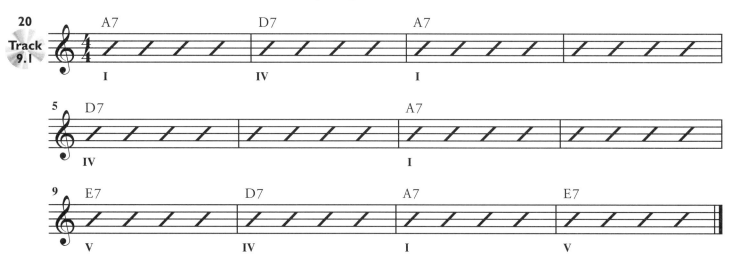

Standard 12-Bar Blues Form with Stops

A *stop* is an accented downbeat followed by a rest, creating a silence for the singer or soloist to fill. In measures 3 and 4, the stops accelerate, creating an exciting rhythm. Elvis Presley's "Jailhouse Rock" and "Blue Suede Shoes" both use this form.

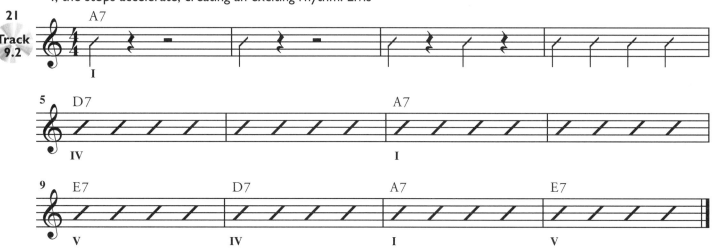

The Simplified 12-Bar Blues Form

This variation omits the chord changes in measures 10 and 12. The simplified form is often used for faster songs where changing chords every measure would be distracting. Chuck Berry's "Johnny B. Goode" uses this form for the chorus, but varies it by adding stops in the solo sections, and his "Roll Over Beethoven" adds the quick change to the IV chord in the 2nd bar.

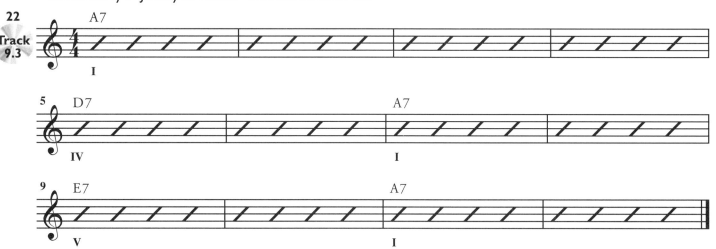

Shuffle Riffs

Now that you know a few blues forms, it's time to play through them with shuffle riffs. This swingin' style will give you a first taste of real blues playing. Here's one simple technique that can work over A7, E7 or D7, by moving it to different strings.

Swing Eighths

Swing Eighths indicates that all eighth notes should be played with a triplet feel (see Tuplets, page 126):

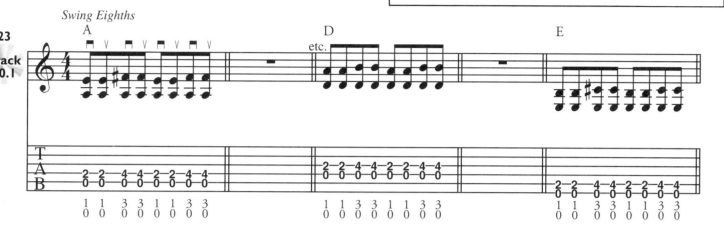

These *closed position* shuffle riffs are *movable* because they don't use open strings. Depending on which fret they're placed, they can be played over any 7th chord. The lowest pitched note is the root note, which determines the letter name of each riff. For example, to use the first riff over a G7 chord, move it to the 3rd fret of the 6th string.

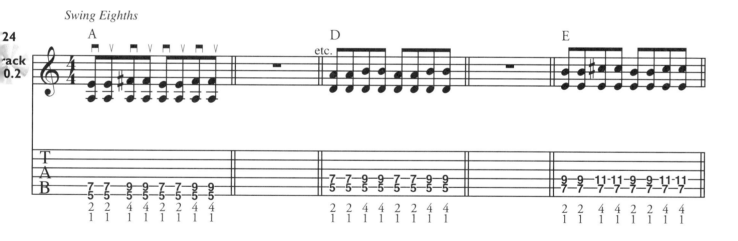

These *inverted* (see page 119) shuffle riffs are also movable, but the higher note is the root note.

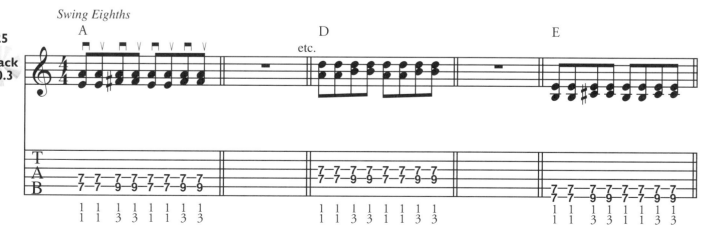

Playing Shuffle Blues

Now, we're going to jump back to pages 25 and 26 and learn to play each form with shuffle riffs. Try the easy riffs from Example 23 first. Each riff has a letter name, as does each bar in the form. Just follow the form bar-by-bar, and you'll have played a shuffle blues. This will take a bit of practice.

After you've mastered the easy shuffle riffs in Example 23, move on to the trickier ones in Examples 24 and 25. You will have to position these according to their root notes as described on page 27. But, the *template method* below will also help you to position the riffs.

I–IV–V Templates

The diagrams below show you how to find root notes for the I–IV–V chords in any key. If the dot representing I is A then the dot representing IV will be D and the dot representing V will be E. If the dot representing I is G then the dot representing IV will be C and the dot representing V will be D, and so on. There are two templates below, each showing a different fretboard relationship of I, IV and V roots.

Root-6 Template

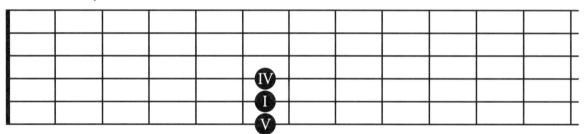

Root-5 Template

Additional note on the 12-bar blues form: The last two bars of the 12-bar form are called the *turnaround*. The purpose of the turnaround is to prepare the listener for the return to the *top* (1st bar) of the 12-bar form. The term *turnaround* also refers to any number of familiar two-bar blues licks that can be inserted in these last two bars.

Also, the 4th bar often includes a *walk-up*, several styles of which are inserted from time to time. A walk-up is a lick used to transition smoothly from the I chord in bars 1 through 4 to the IV chord in bar 5.

This 12-bar blues song includes several types of shuffle riffs, a walk-up and a turnaround. It rolls all of the concepts we've been exploring in this chapter into one cool blues example.

Struttin' Your Stuff

Chucking, Damping and Palm Muting

Chucking

Chucking and *muting* are techniques that can be used in either rhythm or lead guitar. *Rhythm guitar* usually refers to the strumming of chords, and *lead guitar* usually refers to the playing of single-note lines. Chucking results when a guitarist *damps* the strings with his left hand and strums with his right hand, producing a percussive sound. This *chuck* has no specific pitch, so it can blend in with any chord, or over any background.

Damping

To damp the strings with your left hand, simply grasp the neck as if you were fingering a chord and be sure to lightly touch all of the strings so that they are all damped and no notes ring. The following exercises will be a good starting place. More complex chucking examples occur in several upcoming sections.

X = *Chuck,* or percussive sound
with no specific pitch

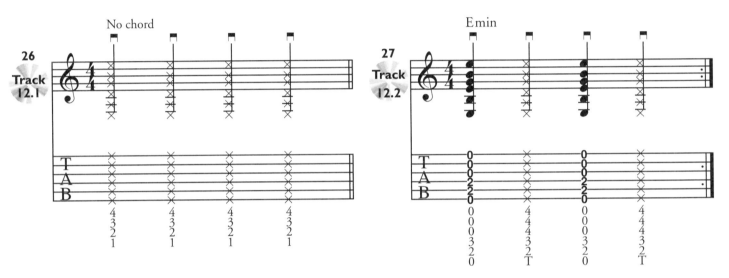

Palm Muting

Palm muting (P.M.) results when the right hand presses lightly against the strings next to the *bridge* (the part of the guitar where the strings are attached to the body; see page 5). Any notes that are picked or strummed should then have a dampened sound. The intensity of the damping effect can be controlled by the pressure against the strings and the distance of the palm from the bridge. This damping effect should not be so strong that the pitches of the notes become unclear.

The exercise below combines chucking and palm muting, both of which greatly enhance a simple chord progression. There will be more examples that feature palm muting in upcoming chapters.

P.M. = Palm muting

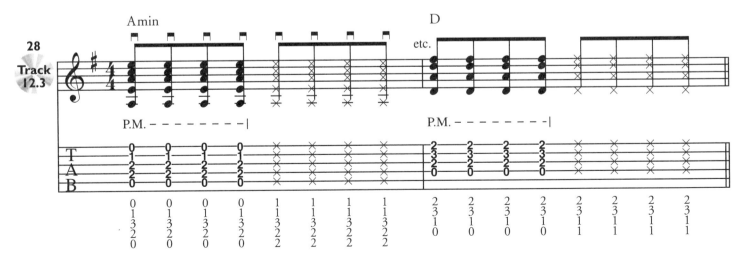

The Art of the Power Chord

Power chords, as defined by *The Total Dictionary of Rock*, are "Crashing, bashing, user-friendly chords that every young rocker hits way too many of when someone in authority needs quiet."

The power chord is technically known as a *5 Chord* because it has only two different notes, the 1st and 5th degrees of the corresponding major scale. They have an extremely strong and stable sound when played loudly with distortion, and blend perfectly with most other chord types.

This is because they don't have either a 3rd or a 7th degree to potentially clash with those of another chord. Also, power chords are a good intermediate step between learning open position chords and barre chords.

The movable power chord shapes below are in *root position*, which means that the lowest pitched note in the chord is the root note, and determines the letter name of the chord. Because these chord shapes are movable, no fret numbers are indicated.

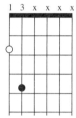   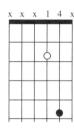 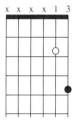

○ = Root note

The forms below add the octave of the root, so you have the 1st, 5th and 8th scale degrees.

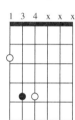 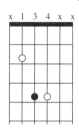 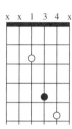 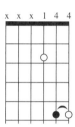

These movable power-chord shapes are inverted, which means that the lowest pitched note in the chord is the 5th, and the letter name of the chord is determined by the indicated root note. You can think of the last one as the *super power chord*. It's a monster.

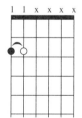   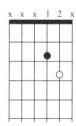  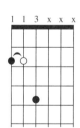 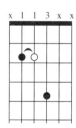

The Super Power Chord

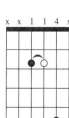 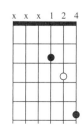  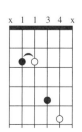 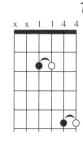 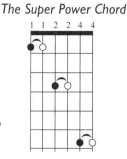

These next chords are not technically power chords because they contain the major 3rd and root of the corresponding major scale. As you already know, a power chord contains only the root and 5th. To make matters more interesting, the lowest note in these shapes is always the 3rd, which makes them inverted.

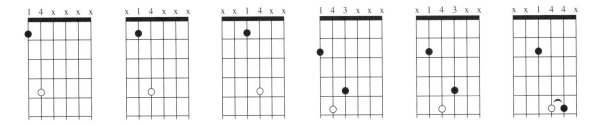

So far, all of the power chords we've learned have been movable, but 5 chords can also contain open strings. Angus Young, of AC/DC, uses this concept very effectively. After all, any of the open strings can act as the root or 5th of a power chord. Below, you'll find some open-string power chords with which to experiment.

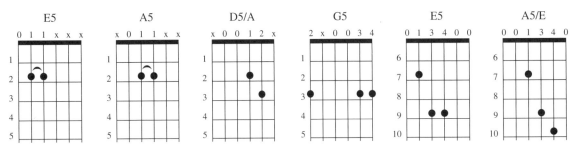

The example below is a very basic power-chord riff. It sounds great with lots of distortion, which you can achieve using a distortion pedal or your amplifier's gain control.

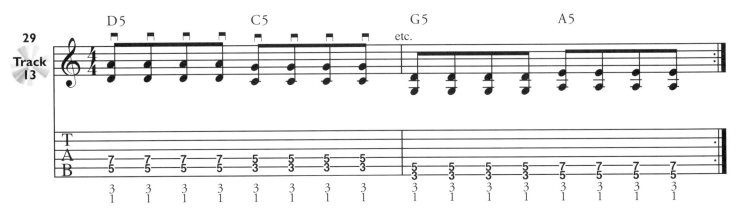

This heavy metal riff includes a *pedal tone* (a note repeated throughout a passage). It also introduces *slides* (see page 60) and palm muting. In bar 2, there is a 5 chord that slides down one fret, and in bar 4 it slides up two frets. Maintain pressure against the fretboard while sliding, so the notes don't fade out.

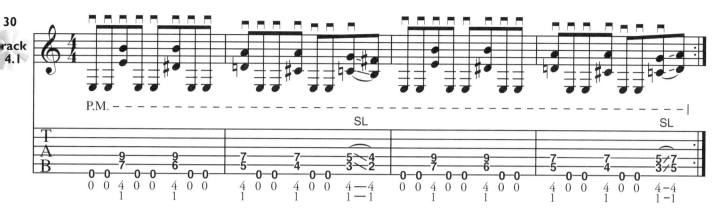

This punk rock riff uses three-note power chords, slides, and chucks (see page 30).

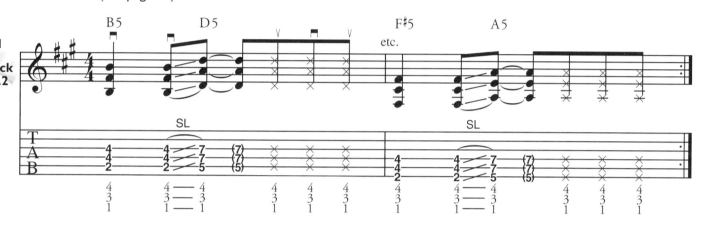

This advanced riff is in the style of Steve Vai or Joe Satriani, and combines slides, chucks, hammer-ons and unusual shapes.

The Art of the Barre Chord

A *barre chord* is one in which a finger forms a straight barre across some or all of the strings, and the other fingers fill out the rest of the notes in the chord. We are about to learn two steps, 1) the *full barre* and, 2) the *E-form barre chord*. The pictures below will help.

The Full Barre

To form the full barre place the 1st finger all the way across the 5th fret of your guitar. Roll the finger slightly, so the left edge of the finger is in contact with the strings. This will work better than the soft underside of the finger. Try to get all of the notes to ring out clearly.

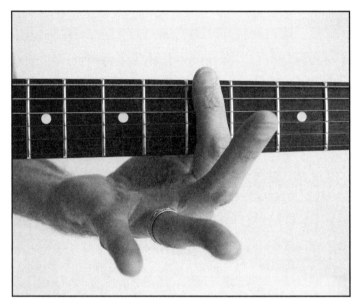

The full barre.

E-Form Barre Chord

E shape or *E form* means it is a common open E chord form moved up to another fret and re-fingered as a barre chord with the indicated root note of the chord determining its letter name. For example, if you place the barre across the 5th fret, the root is an A, so it is now an A chord instead of an E chord. Try to get all of the notes to ring out clearly.

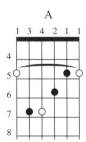

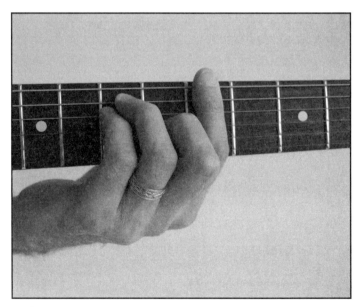

E-form barre chord.

Nine Movable Chords

The box below is a systematic introduction to barre chords. The idea here is to have access to three movable versions of the major triad, minor triad and dominant 7th chord types. These three types are the most commonly played in rock, blues and popular music. They're all based on the open position E, A and D chord forms and their parallel minor and 7th forms. A *parallel* minor is a minor scale (see pages 113 and 122) formed on the same root as the first chord. So, a motion from E to E Minor is a motion from E to its parallel minor. After you have mastered this system, you'll be able to play three different versions of any major, minor or 7th chord, choosing a voicing that best suits your purpose.

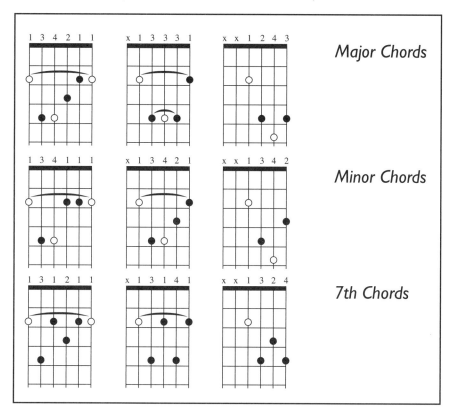

Let's try using the system. We're going to play three E♭ minor chords in ascending order, so that the root notes are all on E♭, like this.

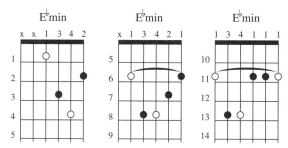

Let's try it again, but with three G7 chords. Do you see how it works? You should be able to do this with any major, minor or 7th chord.

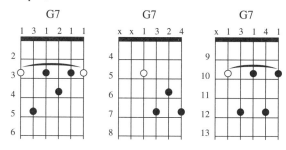

The CAGED Sequence of Barre Chords

The great jazz guitarist Joe Pass lectured eloquently on the *CAGED sequence.** He said that he used the five basic chord types, C, A, G, E and D, to derive all of his other scales and chords. He then demonstrated how everything he played was based around one of the five basic chord forms, how they can be easily morphed to other tonalities like minor, 7th or diminished, and how they move in sequence up the neck, following the CAGED order.

Try the three exercises below to begin familiarizing yourself with this system, which is commonly used for chords, scales and arpeggios. Play each line of five chords repeatedly, until you understand the sequence and how it relates to the open chords. Strum each line of chords freely. Be sure to check the numbers next to the diagrams in the 2nd and 3rd exercises, so you're positioned at the correct frets.

1) Basic open chord CAGED sequence.

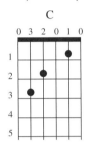 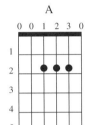  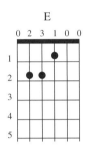 

2) CAGED sequence in D Major, with barre chords. These are barred versions of chords in exercise 1 above.

  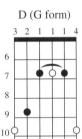 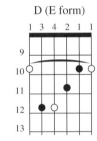 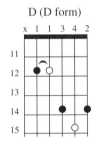

3) CAGED sequence in the key of G Major, with barre chords

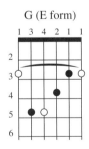 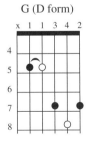 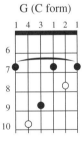 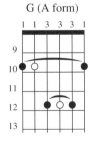 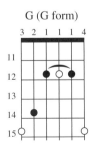

Please notice how each barre chord shape is clearly based on the corresponding open chord shape. Also, notice how the sequence does not always start on C. It can start on any of the five letters, so, it can be: CAGED, AGEDC, GEDCA, EDCAG or DCAGE. There will be more on CAGED sequence scales and arpeggios in several other sections of this book.

* Check out the DVD *An Evening with Joe Pass* (Alfred #0-905013).

This type of passage has been used by artists like Led Zeppelin, David Bowie and The Cure. It's a good introduction to barre-chord riffing.

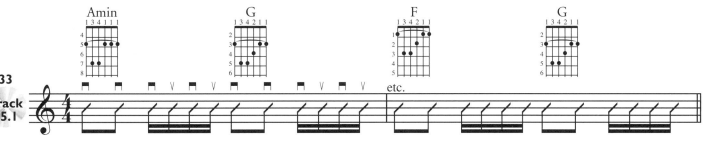

This "ballad" should be played at a slower tempo, and uses some more unusual shapes.

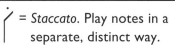

= *Staccato*. Play notes in a separate, distinct way.

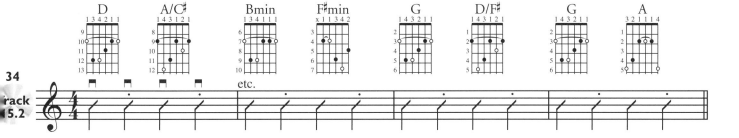

This example expresses the same simple progression in several different ways, encouraging you to use shapes that are rooted on the D string rather than only the E and A strings.

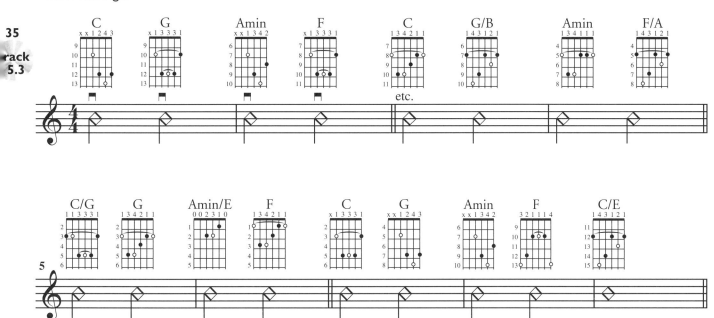

Chord Fragmentation

Any chord can be broken into *fragments*, which are also called *partial chords*. These two- to four-note chords may be formed on adjacent or non-adjacent strings. The common A Major barre chord that you see below can be broken into many fragments, some of which are shown. When playing a partial chord, it's important to use the indicated fingerings and to strum the correct strings. This will help introduce the fragment as a separate chord voicing, with its own shape and fingering.

A Major Barre Chord

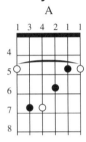

A Major Chord Fragments

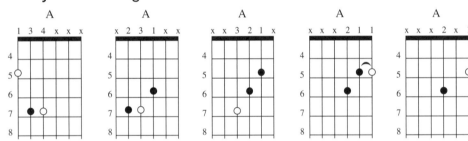

Let's look at fragmenting an A Minor barre chord.

A Minor Barre Chord

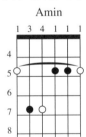

A Minor Chord Fragments

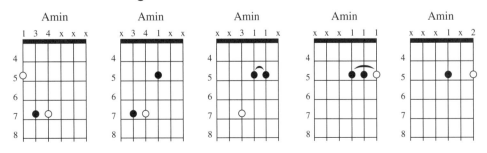

These are the *block chords* (plain, simple chords that are the underlying harmony of a riff or melody) of a common rock chord progression. I–V, then another I–V a whole step lower. Songs such as Bob Dylan's "Lay Lady Lay," Phish's "Sample in a Jar" and TLC's "Waterfalls" use this basic type of progression.

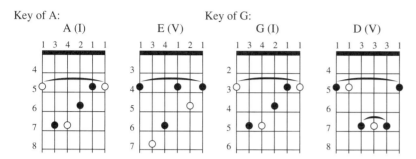

These chords are fragments of the above chords. Two different fragments are shown for the G and D chords.

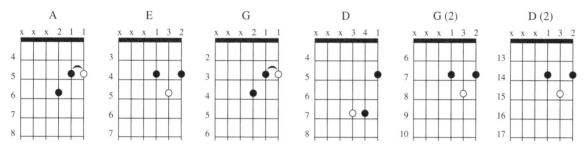

Below is a riff that features the fragments above. Observe the evolution from block chord to fragment to riff. This common and effective device is a key ingredient in many important rock guitar arrangements.

Funkin' with Fragments

Chord fragments can sound notoriously funky, so while we're on the topic, here are a few funky rhythm guitar riffs. Pay close attention to the pick strokes and fingerings. The syncopated rhythms you'll encounter in these examples will be the most challenging yet, so get ready for some serious woodshedding!

Funkin' for the Thrill

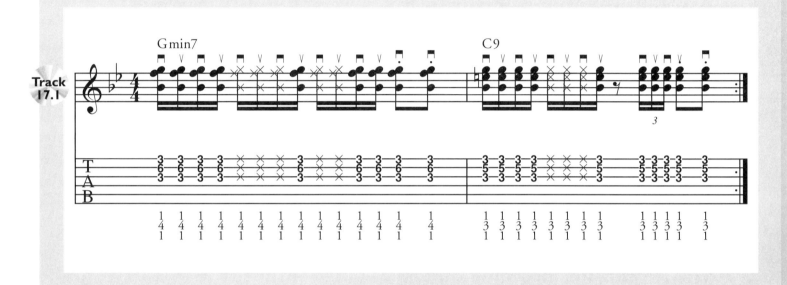

Exit the Zone of Zero Funkativity

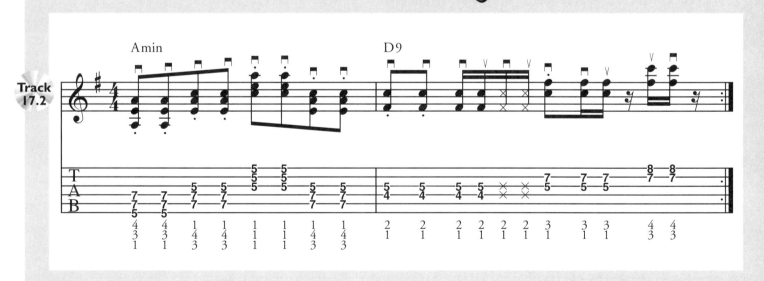

Chord Ornamentation (Hendrix Style)

This chapter is all about that sweet and soulful rhythm guitar sound we all know and love, which is often simply called "Hendrix fills," but is technically known as *chord ornamentation*. Hendrix tunes like "Little Wing," "The Wind Cries Mary" and "Spanish Castle Magic" prominently feature this technique. The Red Hot Chili Peppers based "Under the Bridge" around it, and every advanced rocker should know how to do it.

The idea is to take normal barre-chord forms and play around with their fragments, mixing them with hammer-ons and pull-offs, creating cool little harmonized melodies.

These diagrams show the evolution of an E-form barre chord to fragments to the ornaments around the fragments.

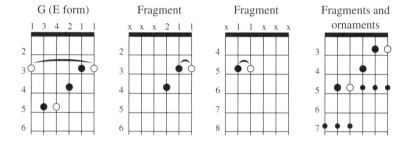

This example shows how to ornament the E-form barre chord, which is being formed on the 3rd fret in the key of G Major.

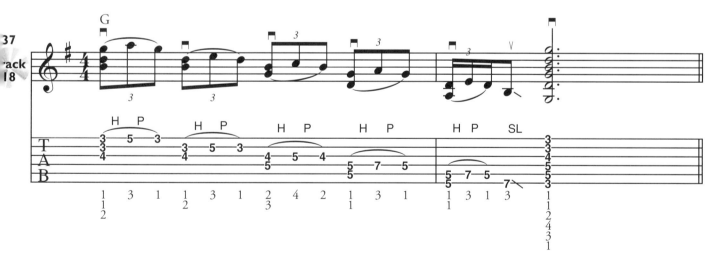

These diagrams show an E Minor-form barre chord and the ornaments around the fragment.

Gmin (Emin form)

Chord and ornaments

This example shows how to ornament the E Minor-form barre chord, which is being formed on the 3rd fret in the key of G Minor.

♪ = *Grace note*. A note with no rhythmic value of its own, which acts as an ornament to the note that follows.

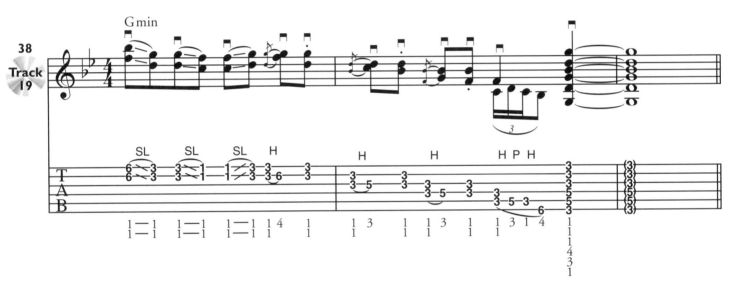

These diagrams show the evolution of an A-form barre chord, from barre chord to fragment to ornamented fragment.

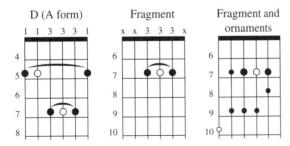

D (A form)

Fragment

Fragment and ornaments

This example shows how you can ornament the A-form barre chord, which is being formed on the 5th fret, in the key of D Major.

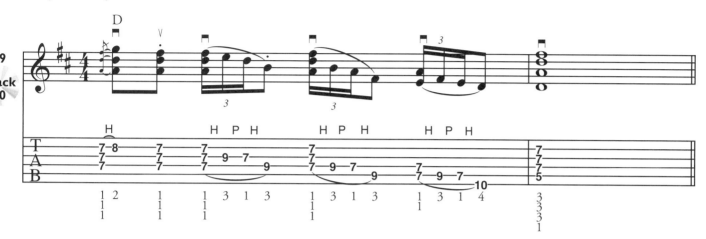

These diagrams show an Amin7-form barre chord and the ornaments around it.

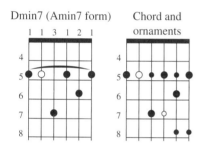

Dmin7 (Amin7 form)   Chord and ornaments

Jimi Hendrix *(1942–1970) is the definitive icon of 1960s rock guitar. In his brief career, he pushed the boundaries of studio recording and live performance years ahead of his time. Heavy distortion, feedback and other effects were a key element of his guitar sound. His music combined the powerful, earthy sounds of blues, jazz and funk with the outer-space sounds of psychedelic rock. Hendrix also left a substantial legacy as a singer, songwriter and cultural figure.*

This example shows how you can ornament the Amin-form barre chord, which is being formed on the 5th fret, in the key of D minor.

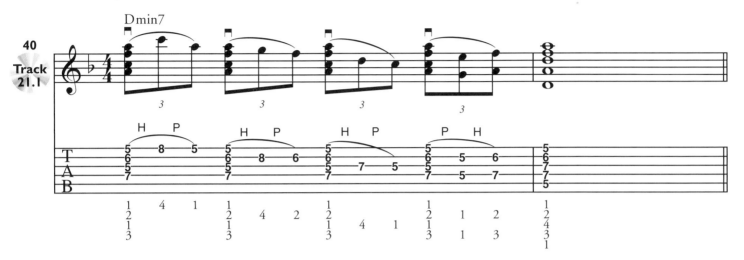

Now that you've learned several ways of ornamenting major and minor chords, you can apply these techniques to chord progressions. This etude is an example of mixing different chord forms and Hendrix fills together to play a I–V–vi–IV progression in the key of G Major. There are a lot of tricky rhythms in this example, including sextuplets (see page 126) and thirty-second note triplets. Thirty-second notes are half the value of sixteenth notes. Two thirty-second notes would equal one quarter of a beat. A thirty-second note triplet is three thirty-second notes in the time of two.

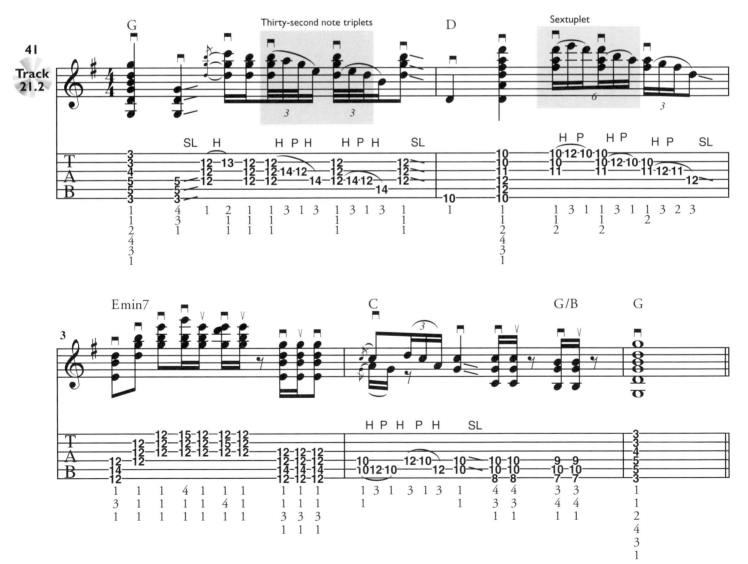

Fingerstyle

The softer side of rock music is often expressed by losing the pick entirely and playing fingerstyle. This is most often done on the acoustic steel-string guitar, but it also occurs on electric and on nylon-string guitar as well. Songs like "Dust in the Wind" by Kansas, "Landslide" by Fleetwood Mac and "Dee" by Randy Rhoads are all classic examples of fingerstyle rock songs.

First, let's get into labeling the right-hand fingers and thumb. The list below and photo to the right show what each finger is named, and why.

These are the Spanish terms, which are typically used in classical guitar notation.

- (*p*) Pulgar — Thumb
- (*i*) Indice — Index
- (*m*) Medio — Middle
- (*a*) Anular — Ring
- (*c*) Chico — Pinky

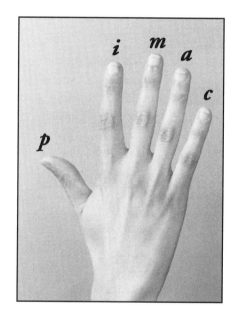

When playing fingerstyle, certain rules, as seen below, tell which fingers hit which strings.

- (*p*) is used for all notes on strings 4, 5 and 6.
- (*i*) is used for all notes on the 3rd string.
- (*m*) is used for all notes on the 2nd string.
- (*a*) is used for all notes on the 1st string.
- (*c*) is not used.

From time to time, at the discretion of the player, these rules may be bent or broken a bit. But, the examples in this book will follow the rules, and if you master them, you'll have a good understanding of real fingerstyle technique.

The exercises that follow will build the fingerstyle skills you'll need to play your favorite fingerstyle rock songs.

This example is a simple introduction to fingerstyle playing.
Make sure you use the correct fingers on each string.

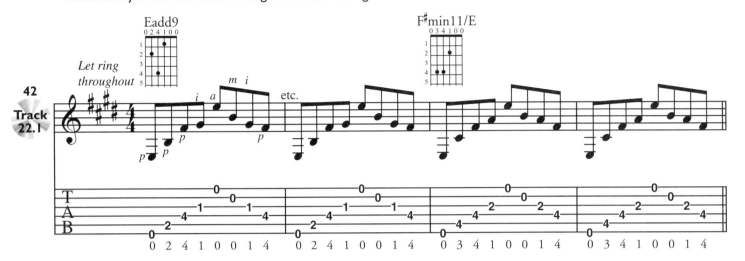

This example introduces a slightly more challenging
pattern, and a common high G pitch in each chord.

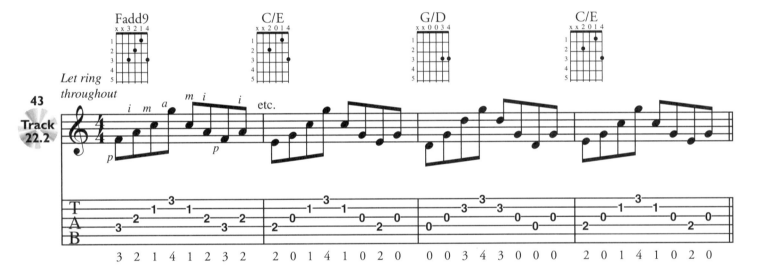

This example is in the style of Fleetwood Mac's "Landslide."

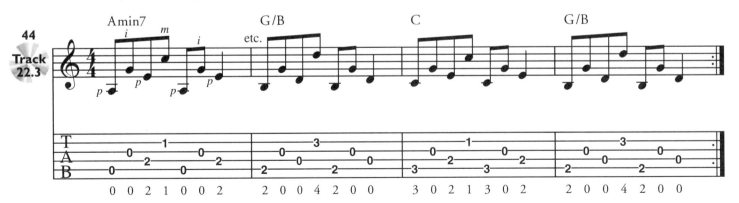

This example introduces the *pinching* technique heard in the beginning of "Stairway to Heaven" and "Dust in the Wind." In this case, pairs of notes are sounded simultaneously throughout the example. Make sure that you're using the correct fingers to pinch. The pinched notes aren't always on the same pair of strings.

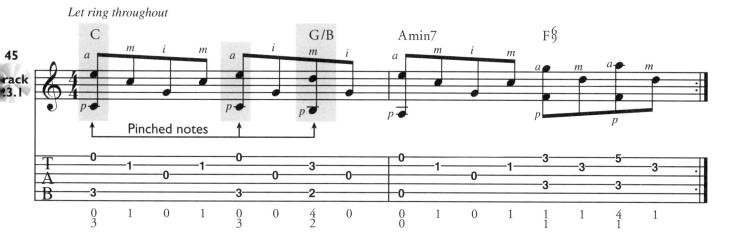

The example below introduces a sixteenth-note pattern. Some interesting chords are used and the pinching technique is revisited. As always, double check your fingerings.

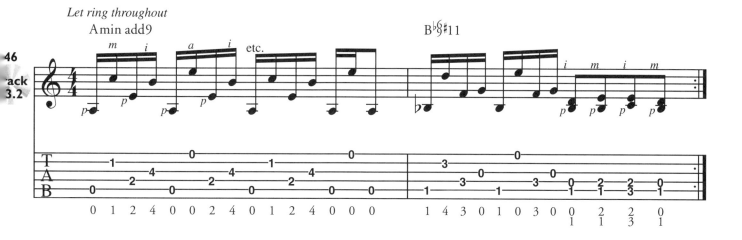

Chord Scales

Diatonic harmony is initially learned on guitar by mastering *chord scales*. The idea is to build a diatonic triad on each degree of the major scale, and to play the scale with triads instead of single notes. This page presents triad scales in open position, and also with roots on the E, A and D strings.

You should master all of the scales on this page and study the theory chapter on page 112 for a better understanding of diatonic harmony. As you play each chord, think of its name and the scale degree on which it is built.

C Major Triad Scale in Open Position

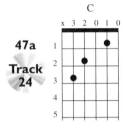 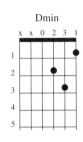 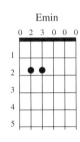 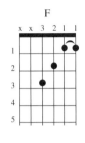   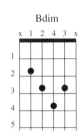 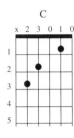

C Major Triad Scale with Roots on the 5th String

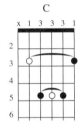 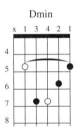 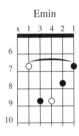 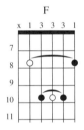 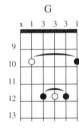 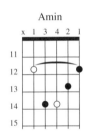 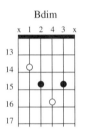 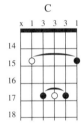

F Major Triad Scale with Roots on the 6th String

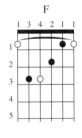    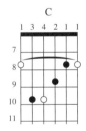 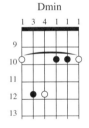 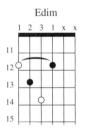 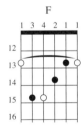

E Major Triad Scale with Roots on the 4th String

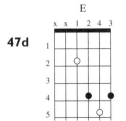 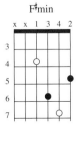  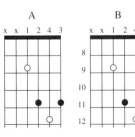 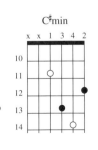 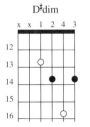 

Chord scales can also be constructed using 7th chords. These scales should be studied and mastered like the ones on page 48.

F Major—7th Chord Scale with Roots on the 6th String

    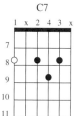  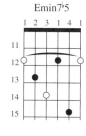 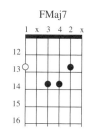

B♭ Major—7th Chord Scale with Roots on the 5th String

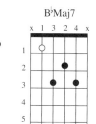 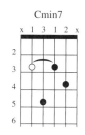 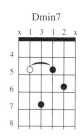 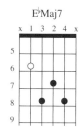 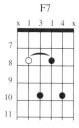  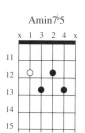 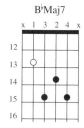

E Major—7th Chord Scale with Roots on the 4th String

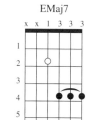  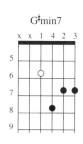   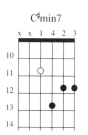 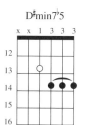 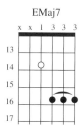

This one mixes triads and 7th chords, and also uses roots on the 6th, 5th and 4th strings. This mixing of chord types and roots allows the scale to stay in one position, rather than climbing the neck.

Chord Scale in A Major

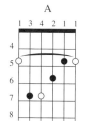  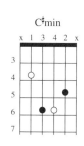  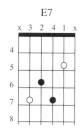 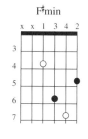 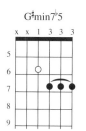 

Once the chord scales on pages 48 and 49 have been mastered, you can easily play numbered chord sequences in any key. In Nashville, this is called the *Nashville numbering system*. Sometimes it's easier to refer to a chord progression as a series of numbers than to specifically name each chord. The upper case Roman numerals are always used for the *primary chords* (chords built on the 1, 4 and 5 of the major scale), and the lower case ones are used for the *secondary chords* (chords built on the 2, 3, 6 and 7 of the major scale). This also develops the ability to hear numbered chord progressions and recognize them by ear, which is a very important skill.

The following chord progressions are all important building blocks of various musical styles. You should memorize the numbered sequence of each one and its unique sound.

49
Track 26.1

Progression 1

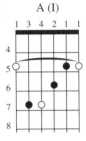 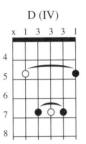 

50
Track 26.2

Progression 2

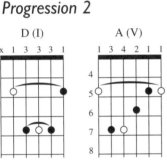 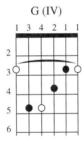 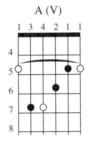

51
Track 26.3

Progression 3

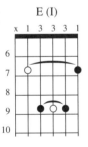 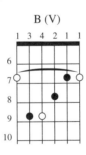 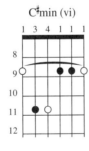 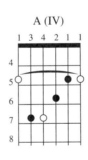

52
Track 26.4

Progression 4

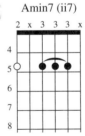 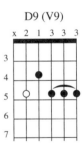

53
Track 26.5

Progression 5

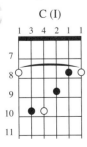  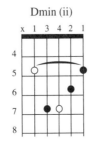 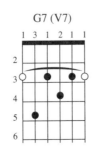

PART 3: Melody and Lead Guitar

Five Major Scale Forms

The major scale lies at the center of music theory; countless other scales are either compared to or derived from the major scale. That's why we're going to learn it first. All of the other scales you'll learn will make more sense after having studied the major scale. Please read over the theory of the major scale on page 112 before learning these fingerings.

The example below is the E Major scale on the 1st string. You can clearly see the W–W–H–W–W–W–H pattern stretching out over the fretboard when the scale is played on one string.

E Major Scale on 1st String

Each of the five major scale fingerings at the bottom of the page is based on one of the five chord shapes in the CAGED sequence (see page 36) and they move up the neck in that order. Start each scale on the lowest pitched root note, play all of the notes in the pattern and then stop on the same root note. You should also practice playing each scale continuously for a few minutes at a time, starting and stopping on the lowest root note. It's important to pay attention to the root notes and fingerings, so you know where to place the scale in a particular key, and also reinforce the sound of the scale in your ear.

If you don't start on the root, then it's not technically a major scale you're playing. Instead it is called a *mode* (see page 74). You'll notice that each form has a name such as *C Form* or *A Form*. This doesn't mean that is necessarily a C scale or an A scale. It means that the form is related to the C chord shape, or the A chord shape. The letter names of these movable scales are determined by the fret on which they are played. The C Form, for example, becomes an F Major scale if played with the 1st finger on the 5th fret, or a G Major scale with the 1st finger on the 7th fret.

C Form

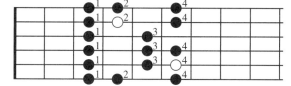

A Form

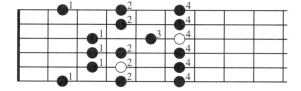

G Form

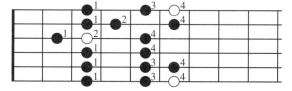

E Form

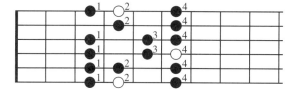

D Form

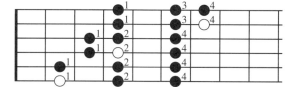

Five Minor Pentatonic Scale Forms

Before starting this section, you may find it helpful to read about minor scale construction (see Minor Key, page 113). The *minor pentatonic scale* is a hugely popular choice when it comes to soloing over a blues or a rock chord progression. Its name comes from combining *penta*, which means "five," and *tonic*, meaning "tone." So, a pentatonic scale is a five-tone scale.

The example below shows the E Minor Pentatonic scale on the 1st string. Its 1½–W–W–1½–W pattern can be clearly seen when we play the scale ascending and descending on one string.

E Minor Pentatonic Scale on 1st String

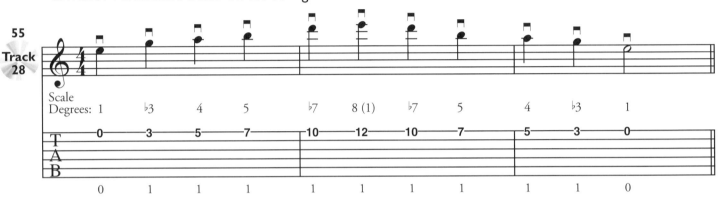

These five minor pentatonic scale fingerings represent the CAGED sequence and should be practiced with attention to the fingerings and root notes, just like the scales on page 51.

C Form
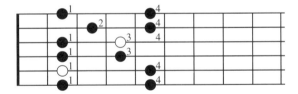

E Form
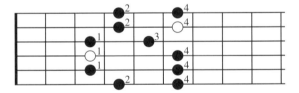

A Form
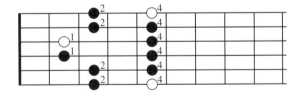

D Form
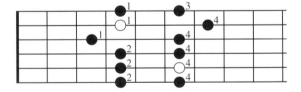

G Form
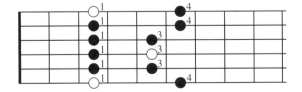

Five Blues Scale Forms

The *blues scale* is almost always interchangeable with the minor pentatonic scale, so it is also a very popular choice when it comes to soloing over a blues or rock progression. The two scales are identical except that the blues scale adds an additional note between the 4th and 5th. So, instead of a five-note scale, it's a six-note scale that includes the ♭5th. The ♭5th is a unique and dissonant sound that is an important part of the blues. Please study the theory on page 112 to fully understand the construction and spelling of the blues scale.

The example below shows the E Blues scale on the 1st string. Its 1½–W–H–H–1½–W pattern can be clearly seen when we play the scale ascending and descending on one string.

The E Blues Scale on 1st String

56

Track 29

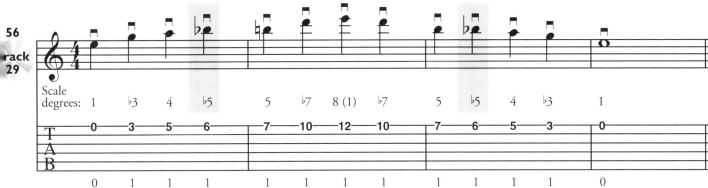

These five blues scale fingerings represent the CAGED Sequence and should be practiced with attention to the fingerings and root notes, just like the scales on page 51.

C Form

E Form

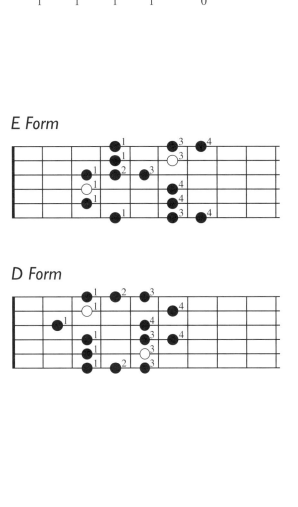

A Form

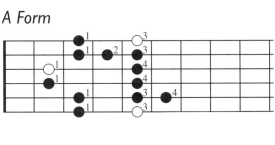

D Form

G Form

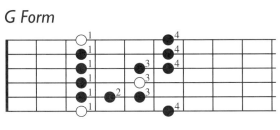

Five Major Pentatonic Scale Forms

The *major pentatonic scale* is very useful for playing rock, country and blues. Like the minor pentatonic, it is a five-tone scale. Please study the theory on page 112 to fully understand the construction and spelling of the major pentatonic scale.

This example shows the E Major Pentatonic scale on the 1st string. Its W–W–1½–W–1½ pattern can be clearly seen when we play the scale ascending and descending on one string.

The E Major Pentatonic Scale on 1st String

You will immediately notice that these five patterns below are exactly the same as the five minor pentatonic patterns on page 52, except that their root notes are three frets higher, matching those of the corresponding CAGED chord shape. These five scale fingerings represent the CAGED sequence and should be practiced with attention to the fingerings and root notes, just like the scales on page 51.

C Form

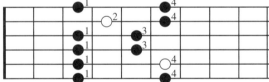

E Form

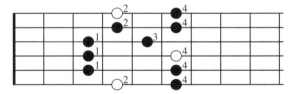

A Form

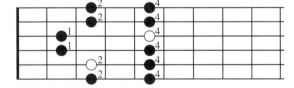

D Form

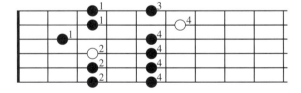

G Form

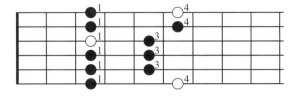

The CAGED Sequence Applied to Scales

A common mistake made by many guitar students is relying too heavily on memorizing fingerings of different scales, chords, licks and songs. Learning by memorization alone works well at first, until the point of critical mass is reached. Then, this type of player becomes frustrated and begins seeking other ways to get to the next level.

With a broader understanding of why things fit together, an eye for recognizing connecting patterns in scale and chord forms and an interest in the theory that ties everything together, it's much easier to make it to the next level.

The diagrams below show the CAGED sequence, first in open chords, then in barre chords, then in minor pentatonic scales, then in major scales. You should trace your eye down each line of grids, think about the patterns you've learned, and really "see" the chord shape within each larger form.

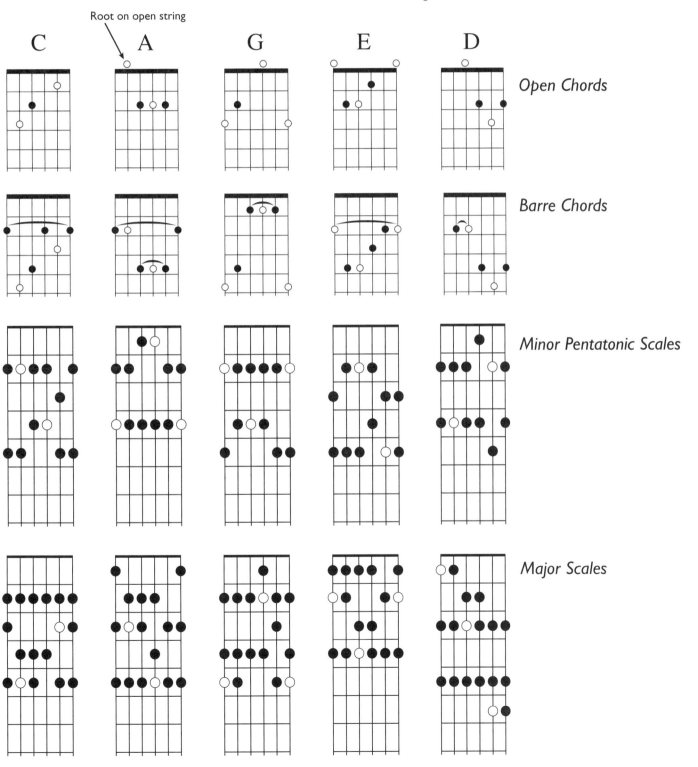

Exotic Scales

Exotic scales are used in rock music to evoke certain moods or "colors" that are not available in common diatonic or blues scales. They aren't used as much as pentatonic scales, blues scales, major scales or diatonic modes, but they can create memorable instrumental "hooks" in songs. The Rolling Stones used the *harmonic minor scale* in "Paint It Black," and the Offspring used the *phrygian dominant scale* in "Come Out and Play." Both choices were very effective. Yngwie Malmsteen, Buck Dharma and Ritchie Blackmore all use various exotic scales when improvising. We're going to introduce some exotic scales in this section, just to familiarize you with their uses in rock music.

Harmonic Minor Scale

Formula: W–H–W–W–H–1½–H
Notes from C root: C–D–E♭–F–G–A♭–B–C
Sound: Has a "Middle Eastern" or "Arabian" sound. Is also used, or perhaps overused, by neo-classical shredders like Joe Stump and Yngwie Malmsteen.
Usage: Works over a minor triad of the same root, or a Dominant 7th chord a 5th higher, for example Cmin or G7.
Comparison: Is exactly the same as a natural minor scale except that it has a ♮7.
Modes: Start it on its 5th degree to create the Phrygian dominant scale.

Harmonic Minor Scale

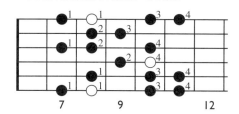

Phrygian Dominant Scale

Formula: H–1½–H–W–H–W–W
Notes from C root: C–D♭–E–F–G–A♭–B♭–C
Sound: Has a "Spanish" sound. Combines characteristics of the harmonic minor scale and the Phrygian mode. The ♭2nd interval creates a very exotic sound.
Usage: Works best over a dominant 7th chord of the same root, or a minor triad a 5th below, such as C7 or Fmin.
Comparison: It's the 5th mode of the harmonic minor scale, and can also be thought of as a Phrygian mode with a ♮3. That's why it's sometimes called the Phrygian natural third scale.

Phrygian Dominant Scale

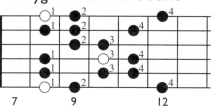

Chromatic Scale

Formula: H–H–H–H–H–H–H–H–H–H–H–H
Notes from C root:
C–C♯–D–D♯–E–F–F♯–G–G♯–A–A♯–B–C
Sound: This multi-purpose scale is used in jazz, surf, classical, shred and many other styles. Its sound depends largely on how it is used. Since it contains all 12 possible tones, it can produce anything from very discordant sounds to pop melodies.
Usage: Works over any chord, and in any key, if resolved properly and played briskly.
Analysis: There is only one chromatic scale. It's a symmetrical scale featuring all 12 tones separated by intervals of one half step.

Chromatic Scale

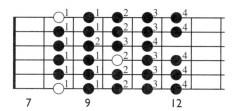

Whole Tone Scale

Formula: W–W–W–W–W–W
Notes from C root: C–D–E–F#–G#–A#–C
Sound: Has an "augmented" sound, due to the #5th interval in the scale. It pops up frequently in jazz and fusion music, but is also heard in classical, rock and even blues.
Usage: Works best over augmented triads and dominant 7th #5 chords such as Caug or C7#5.
Analysis: This scale features six notes separated by intervals of one whole step. There are only two different whole tone scales, because each one of them features six of the 12 possible tones.

Whole Tone Scale

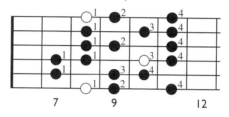

Diminished Half–Whole Scale

Formula: H–W–H–W–H–W–H–W
Notes from C root: C–D♭–E♭–E–G♭–G–A–B♭–C
Sound: Has an "altered" (modern jazz) type of sound.
Usage: It works well over diminished 7th chords and diminished triads. It also works over *altered dominants* (see page 116) such as the 7♭9, 7♭5, and 7#9, or double altered chords containing combinations of ♭9, #9 and ♭5. For example, C7♭9♭5.
Analysis: This is an eight-note scale with an alternating pattern of half steps and whole steps.

Diminished Half-Whole Scale

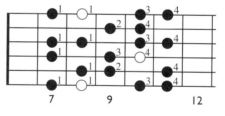

Diminished Whole–Half Scale

Formula: W–H–W–H–W–H–W–H
Notes from C root: C–D–E♭–F–G♭–A♭–A–B–C
Sound: Has a "jazz minor" type of sound.
Usage: It works well over diminished 7th chords and diminished triads, for example Cdim7.
Analysis: This is an eight-note scale with an alternating pattern of whole steps and half steps. It's very similar to the melodic minor scale, sharing most of its important characteristics, but adding the ♭5.

Diminished Whole-Half Scale

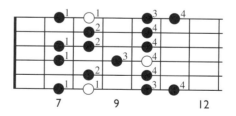

Melodic Minor Scale

Formula: W–H–W–W–W–W–H
Notes from C root: C–D–E♭–F–G–A–B–C
Sound: Is widely called "the jazz minor scale" because this nickname describes its sound.
Usage: This scale is mostly used to cover the altered tones in altered dominant chords one half step below its root. In other words: play a C Melodic Minor scale over an B7♭9 chord. It also works well over min/Maj7 chords.
Comparison: It's exactly the same as a common major scale, but has a minor 3rd.
Modes: Start it on its 7th degree to create the Super Locrian mode. Start it on its 4th degree to create the Lydian ♭7 mode.

Vibrato

Vibrato is the art of warbling the pitch of a note or group of notes to achieve a musical effect. It can be done by gently and rhythmically depressing your whammy bar a slight amount (if you have a whammy bar) and it can also be done by using any of four vastly different finger techniques. These are called: *rock vibrato, classical vibrato, bending rock vibrato* and *circular vibrato*.

Rock Vibrato

This is the very wide and wild style of vibrato that we see Jimmy Page using in film footage of Led Zeppelin. The idea is to finger a single note with the left-hand 3rd finger. Then, rock the wrist in such a way as to cause that finger to tug down on the string and then push it back up, bending it slightly up in pitch, as the note sustains. The note will move through three positions in a rhythmic cycle. These positions are: 1) static, 2) bent downward and, 3) bent upward. So, the note warbles between its natural pitch and a higher pitch. Try applying rock vibrato to the A note in the following example.

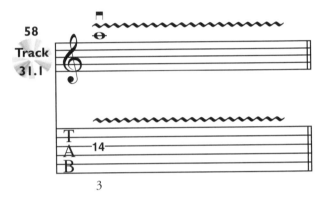

Classical Vibrato

This is the sensitive and expressive style of vibrato that classical guitarists and violinists tend to use. It is achieved by pulling the string to the left and to the right while sustaining a note. Simply sustain the A note in the above example and rock your finger back and forth to the left and right while pressing the note down. As you rock to the left, the note will go sharper in pitch. As you rock to the right, it will go flat. In the middle position the note will be unaffected. The speed and depth of the vibrato can be controlled by the speed and length of the rocking motion. This style of vibrato raises and lowers the original pitch, unlike rock vibrato, which only raises it.

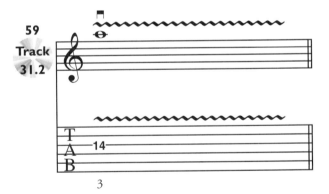

Bending Rock Vibrato

This is the kind of vibrato that Jimi Hendrix always used while bending a screaming note. Virtually all rock and blues players have come to rely on this very expressive technique. After *bending* (page 61) the note, apply rock vibrato by rocking your wrist so the note goes slightly flat and then returns to the true bent pitch in a rhythmic motion. Unlike static rock vibrato, in which the note only goes sharp, this type of vibrato can cause it to go sharp or flat. For now, just let it go flat, then back up to the regular pitch. Practice applying bending rock vibrato to the bend in this example.

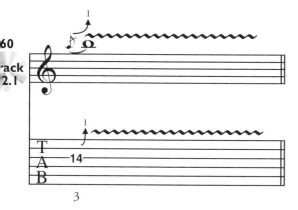

Circular Vibrato

This rare and difficult style of vibrato was invented by Steve Vai. It allows the wildness of rock vibrato and the sensitivity of classical vibrato, by merging the two techniques into one. The idea is to rock your finger back and forth and pull it up and down at the same time, in a circular motion. Let's break it down into steps. Try this on the A note in this example.

1) Rock your finger to the left.
2) Pull your finger down.
3) Push your finger up.
4) Rock your finger to the right.
5) Pull your finger down.

By repeating these steps while holding down a sustained note you can achieve a number of interesting vibrato effects that involve the pitch raising, lowering and returning to normal.

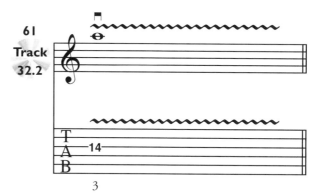

Other Left-Hand Techniques

This chapter will introduce a few common single-string techniques such as *bends, slides, hammer-ons, pull-offs* and *trills*. These are all called *slurs*. Only the first note of a slur is picked by the right hand, and the second note is sounded using the left hand alone. A slur is written in tablature or standard music notation as a curved line ⌒ connecting two or more notes. All of the techniques in this section are needed to become a great rock lead guitarist.

The Hammer-On: A note that is *hammered-on* is not picked. Instead, the sound is created by "hammering" the finger down on the fretboard. Try this: Pluck the open 1st string. Hammer your left-hand 1st finger onto the 2nd fret of the same string. You should hear two notes: the picked E note, followed by the hammered F♯ note. The letter H above a slur indicates a hammer-on.

The Pull-Off: A *pulled-off* note is not picked. The sound is created by pulling another left-hand finger off a fretted note on the same string, which causes the lower pitched note to sound without being picked. Try this: Place your 1st finger on the 2nd fret of the 1st string. Pick the note and then snap your finger off the string by pulling it downward, so that the open-1st string rings without being picked. You should hear two notes, the picked F♯ note and the pulled-off open-E note. The letter P above a slur indicates a pull-off.

The Trill: A *trill* is a rapid and continuous series of hammer-ons and pull-offs. Try this: Place your 1st finger on the 2nd fret A note on the G string. Pick that note and hammer-on to the 4th fret B note of the same string with your 3rd finger. Pull-off to the A note. Continue hammering-on and pulling-off between these two notes. This is trilling. You should not need to pick to maintain the trill. The note you are trilling to is in parentheses (•) and above the staff you will see this indication: *tr*〜〜〜.

The Slide: A note that is *slid* to is sometimes picked and sometimes sounded only by the act of sliding to it. Try this: Pick the A note on the 14th fret of the G string with your 1st finger. While maintaining pressure against the fretboard, slide the same finger to the 16th fret of the same string. You should hear the note A slide up to the note B. The letters SL above a slur and an ascending or descending line indicates a slide.

The Double-Picked Slide: This is when both notes in the slide are picked. Try this: Pick the A note on the 14th fret of the G string with your 1st finger. While maintaining pressure against the fretboard, slide the same finger to the 16th fret of the same string. Pick the B note as soon as you reach it. You should hear the picked A note slide up to the picked B note. The letters SL above an ascending or descending line with no slur indicates a *double-picked slide*.

The Unspecified Slide: This is a slide with no particular destination. Try this: Pick the A note on the 14th fret of the G string with your 1st finger. Move your hand to your left, while maintaining pressure against the fretboard. Gradually decrease the pressure as you keep moving your hand, so that a slide effect is achieved without sliding to a specific note. The letters SL above an ascending or descending line, with no slur or destination note, indicates an *unspecified slide*.

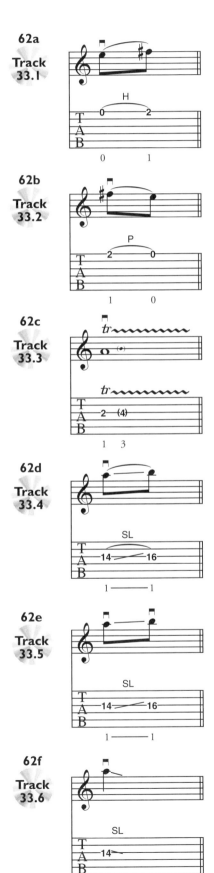

The Bend: To *bend* is to raise the pitch of a fretted note by bending the string. Try this: Place your 3rd finger on the 7th fret D note of the G string. Back it up by placing your 1st and 2nd fingers behind it, on the 5th and 6th frets of the same string. Now pick the G string and push the string upward, while maintaining pressure against the fretboard. The farther you push the string up, the more the note will rise in pitch. The most common distance to bend is one whole step. So, keep pushing until the note reaches E. You can check the E pitch by fingering the 9th fret E note on the G string. You should bend until you match this pitch.

A note can be bent up ½ step, 1 whole step, 1½ steps, 2 steps or more. A curved arrow pointing upward indicates that the note is to be bent. A number such as 1 or ½ indicates how far it is to be bent.

The Reverse Bend: This is when a note is bent before it is picked. It is then picked and released to its normal pitch. This technique is also called the *pre-bend and release*. Try this: Place your fingers in the bending position described in Example 63a. Bend the D note on the 7th fret of the G string up to E without picking it. Pick the string and release the bend so that you hear the note E moving smoothly down one whole step to the note D. An arrow pointing straight up indicates that the note has been pre-bent. The number above the arrow tells how far the note is pre-bent.

The Unison Bend: This is when two notes are fingered and picked simultaneously, and the lower-pitched note is bent to reach the pitch of the higher note while both notes sustain. Try this: Place your 1st finger on the 5th-fret E note of the B string. Place your 3rd finger on the 7th fret D note on the G string. Back the 3rd finger up with your 2nd finger on the 6th fret of the G string. Pick the G and B strings simultaneously with a downstroke, and bend the G string up one whole step to the pitch E. Make sure that both strings ring out, so that you hear both E notes at once after the bend.

The Harmonized Bend: This is when two notes are fingered and picked simultaneously, and the lower-pitched note is bent up to harmonize with the pitch of the higher note while both notes sustain. Try this: Place your 1st finger on the 5th-fret E note of the B string. Place your 4th finger on the 8th-fret G note on the B string. Back the 3rd finger up with your 2nd finger on the 6th fret of the G string. Pick the G and B strings simultaneously with a downstroke and bend the G string up one whole step to the pitch E. Make sure that both strings ring out, so that you hear the bent E note and the G note together after the bend.

The following examples feature these techniques in musical contexts.

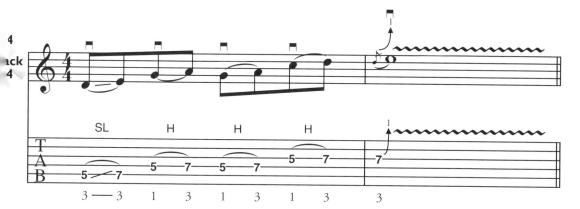

This E Minor pentatonic lick is in the style of Jimi Hendrix. It starts with an unspecified slide, moves into a trill and ends with a unison bend. Try it over an E Minor chord.

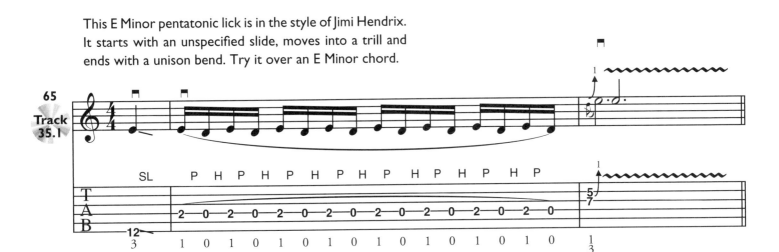

This rockin' lick uses notes from the D Blues scale. It includes pull-offs, hammer-ons and a harmonized bend. Try it over a D5 chord.

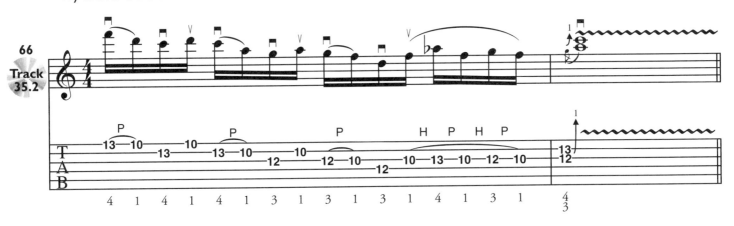

This G Minor Pentatonic riff introduces reverse bends and *double-stop hammer-ons* (simultaneous hammer-ons on two different strings). Try it over a G5.

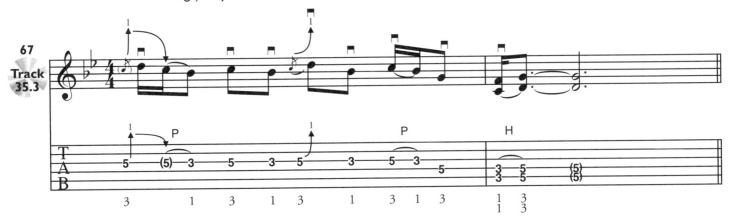

Five-Note Patterns and the Albert King Box

This A Minor Pentatonic scale exercise climbs the neck in identical groups of five notes. These symmetrical groups are G–A–C–D–E. Always slide the D note to the E note when ascending. When descending, the pattern is reversed, so you slide the E down to the D note each time. This sliding is very useful for climbing up and down the neck. This combines notes from four of our five minor pentatonic scale forms into one big form. Many players use this type of scale form almost exclusively when soloing.

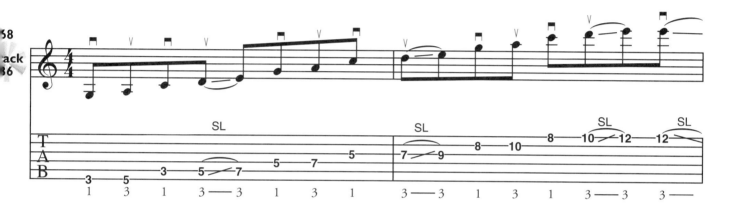

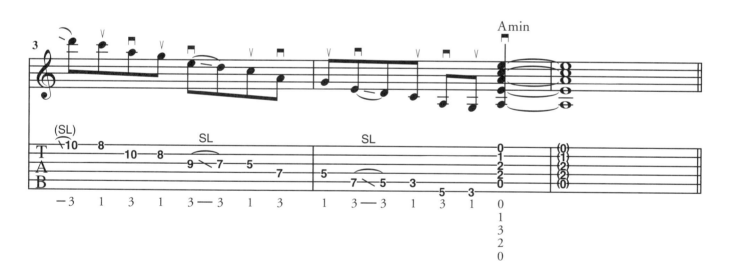

The Albert King Box

This diagram shows *The Albert King Box*. Notice how it isolates five notes from the second bar of the scale exercise above. Countless cool blues/rock riffs can be played using this box alone. In fact, many players restrict themselves to this box while soloing.

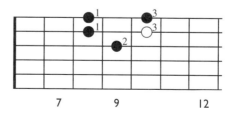

This A Major Pentatonic scale exercise is similar to the A Minor Pentatonic exercise on page 63. It covers a little more area on the neck, but still uses a symmetrical five-note pattern which slides from position to position.

The Albert King Box (Key of A Major)

This Albert King Box is in the key of A Major. You will notice it uses the same scale as Example 69 (A Major Pentatonic), but is played in a different area of the fretboard. Try soloing in A Major and alternating between this box and the pattern above.

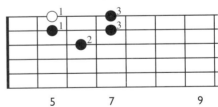

Pentatonic/Blues Lick Index

This collection of licks is a useful resource for building classic rock lead guitar skills. They are all in the key of A Minor, which means that you can play them over the chords: A Minor, C Major and even A7. You can also play them over chord progressions in the key of A Minor or C Major.

You should repeat each lick until it's memorized and flowing smoothly. Then try combining them. Since they are all in the same key, you can combine them in any order you wish. Play one four times, then another, and another. Play half of one, then half of another. You get the idea. Experiment. They're all movable, so you can play them in any key by repositioning them on the fretboard. Many of these licks are in the styles of Jimi Hendrix, Jimmy Page, Ace Frehley, Chuck Berry and countless others. They are repeated from solo to solo by everyone from Slash to Joe Satriani. These licks are the primary vocabulary of rock lead guitar. Learn them well.

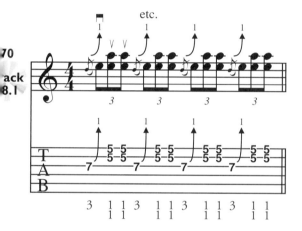

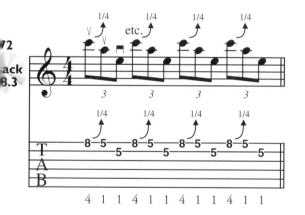

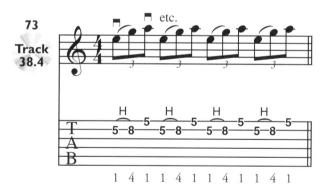

74
Track
39.1

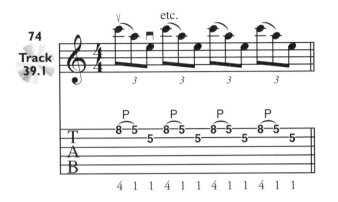

75
Track
39.2

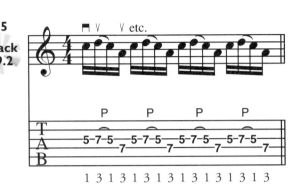

76
Track
39.3

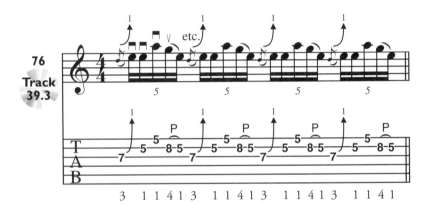

77
Track
39.4

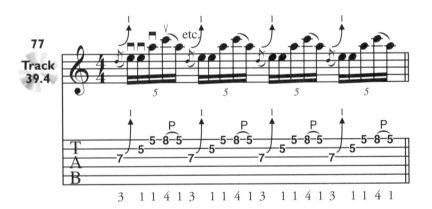

78
Track
39.5

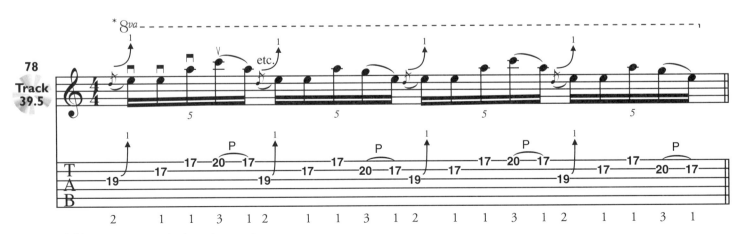

* Play one octave higher than written

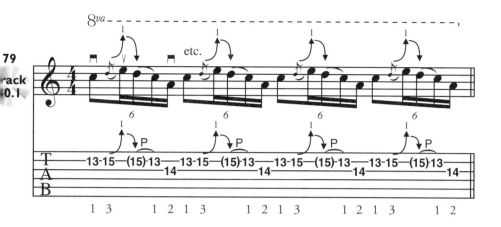

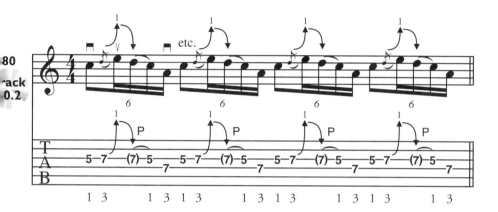

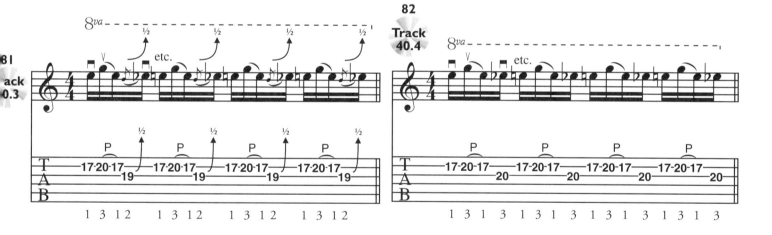

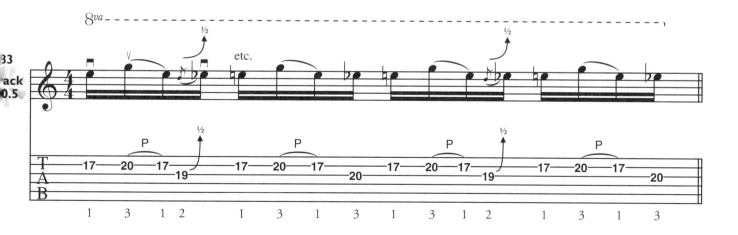

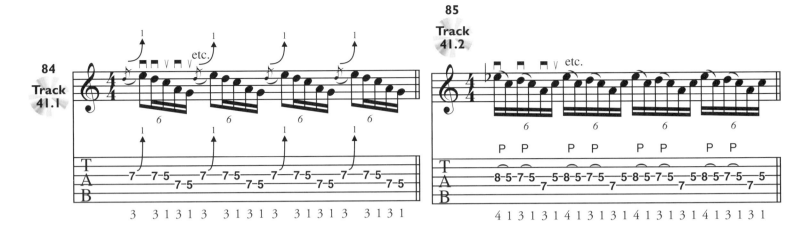

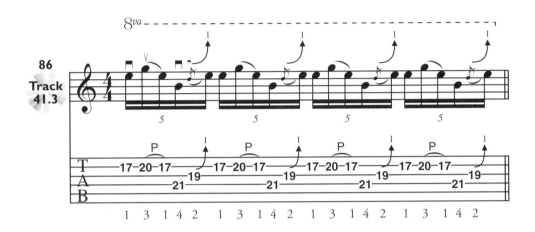

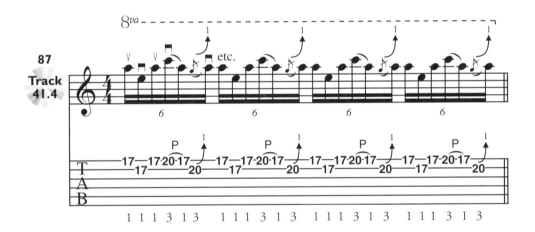

This is a lick from the song "Shred Planet" from *The Way of Zen Guitar*.

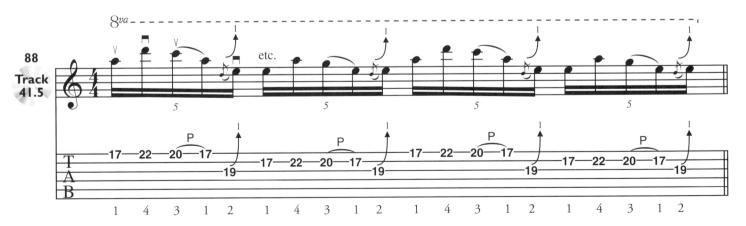

Melodic Patterns

Melodic patterns, also called *scale sequences*, are excellent "chops" builders for guitar, and are also important tools for sight reading, improvisation and ear training. A *sequence* is a pattern of intervals that is repeated starting on different pitches. The idea is to repeat the same pattern while ascending and/or descending through the tones of the scale. An array of instantly recognizable and very musical sounding melodies can be created using this concept. The following is an explanation of a simple melodic pattern in C Major.

These are the notes in a C Major scale with each tone numbered.

C D E F G A B

1 2 3 4 5 6 7

This is a simple sequence, that is commonly called a *threes sequence*.

C–D–E D–E–F E–F–G F–G–A G–A–B A–B–C

1–2–3 2–3–4 3–4–5 4–5–6 5–6–7 6–7–1

It is called a threes sequence because the notes climb the scale in groups of three. Many familiar melodies are created in this way. Metallica frequently applies this sequence to the E Blues scale, which has been jokingly referred to as "the key of Metallica." The example below shows how to play a one-octave threes sequence ascending and descending in C Major. Use the E form of the C Major scale.

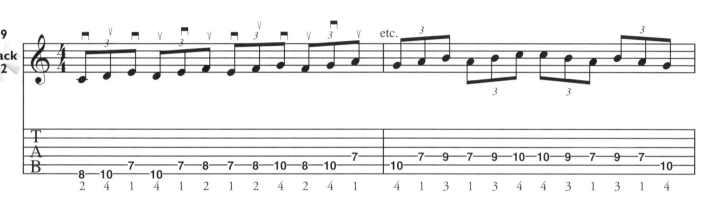

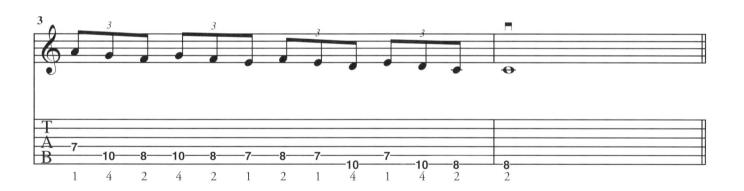

This heavy metal example shows how to play a *fours sequence*, which climbs the A Minor scale (also known as the *A Aeolian mode*, see page 74) in groups of four, then culminates in a screaming bend.

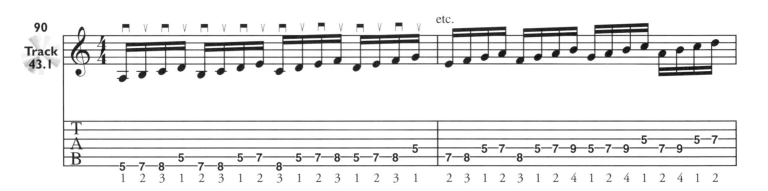

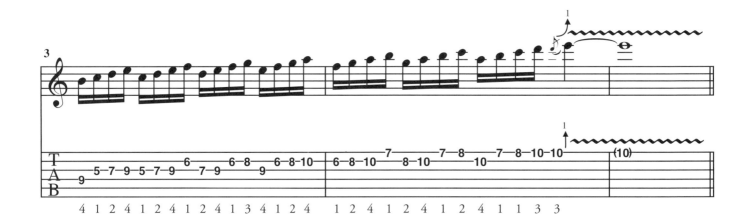

This sequence is called *diatonic thirds*. It climbs the G Major scale in the following manner:

1–3, 2–4, 3–5, 4–6, 5–7, etc.

Use the E form of the G Major scale, starting on the 3rd-fret G note.

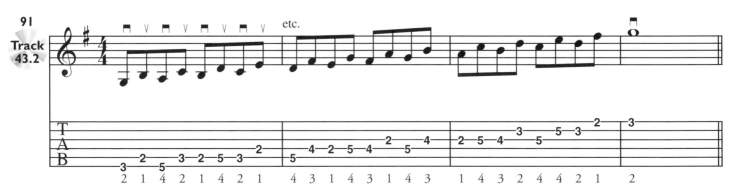

Example 92 is a complex melodic pattern in the style of Steve Vai. It takes 14 notes before this pattern repeats, starting on the next lowest scale tone. It climbs the E Phrygian mode (see page 74) in the following sequence.

1–2–3–4–3–2– 1–2–3–4– 5–6–7–6

5–6–7–8–7–6– 5–6–7–8– 9–10–11–10

9 –10–11–12–11–10– 9 –10–11–12–13–14–15–14

This E Phrygian fingering is a "long scale," spanning the open 6th string to the 12th fret of the 1st string. There's an *accent* (a note played louder than the others) at the beginning of each new melodic pattern. Notice how this accent never occurs in the same place within any bar. This changing accent creates a mesmerizing and unpredictable effect of "dancing around the beat."

> = accent

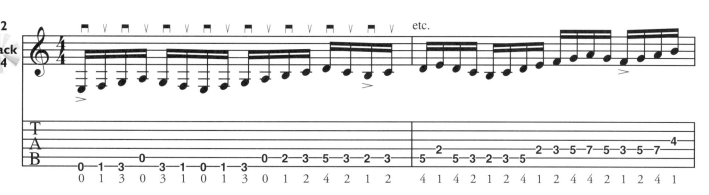

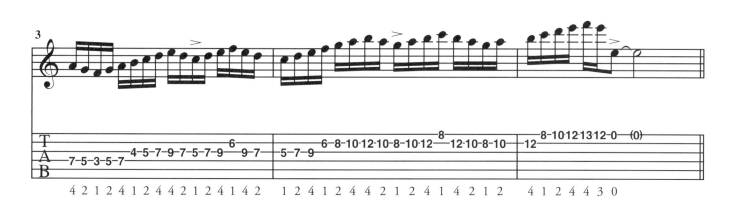

This is a tried and true B *Locrian* (see page 74) shred
sequence in the style of Paul Gilbert of Racer X. It should
be played as fast as possible…no…faster than possible.

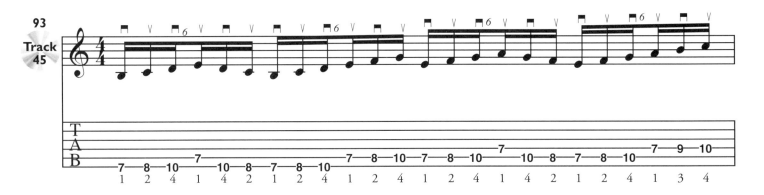

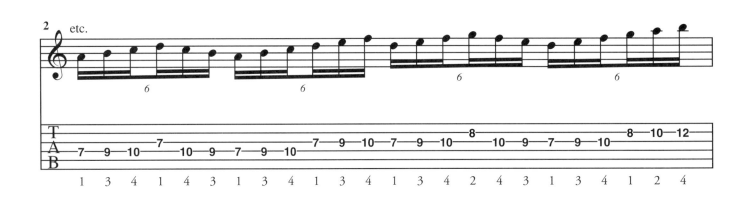

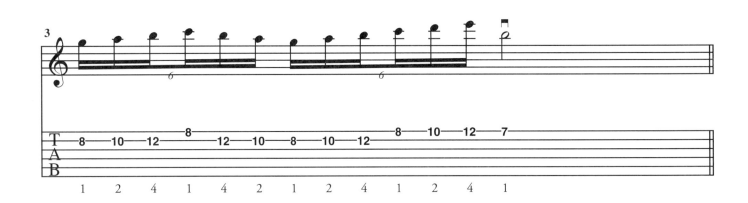

This example is the same type of sequence as Example 93, but descending. Notice that the alternate picking is reversed, so that it starts on an upstroke, instead of a downstroke. This facilitates easy *string shifts* throughout the sequence. For more on string shifting, see the Speed Picking chapter on page 109.

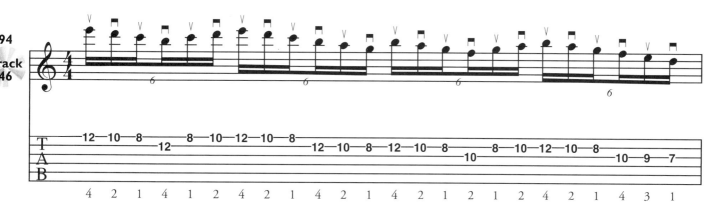

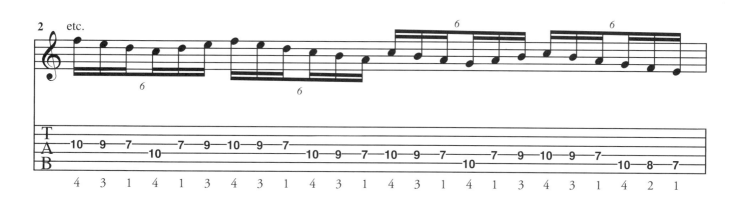

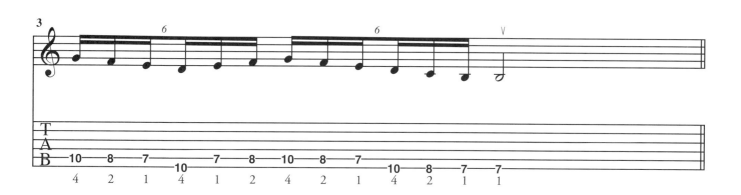

Modes

It's time to explore the intriguing world of *modes*. Modes have fancy names like E♭ Mixolydian, C#Phrygian and D Lydian. Sophisticated players like Frank Zappa and Steve Vai have used them in their solos and discussed them in interviews. So, it only makes sense that you should be equally able to play cool modal solos and impress your peers.

In a nutshell; the modes are a way of shifting the root note of the common major scale to create a new scale. (If you are not thoroughly familiar with major scale theory, review page 112.) Here's how it works: There are seven different notes in each major scale. Below, you see the notes of the C Major scale spelled out.

C–D–E–F–G–A–B–C

By rearranging the major scale to start on a different root note, you can create seven different modes. Each of these seven modes has a different Greek name.

C	D	E	F	G	A	B	C	C Ionian
	D	E	F	G	A	B	C	D	D Dorian
		E	F	G	A	B	C	D E	E Phrygian
			F	G	A	B	C	D E F	F Lydian
				G	A	B	C	D E F G	G Mixolydian
					A	B	C	D E F G A	A Aeolian
						B	C	D E F G A B	B Locrian

Note that the Ionian mode is the same as the major scale and that the Aeolian mode is precisely the same as the relative minor (also called the natural minor scale, see page 113). This procedure can be done in any key. To the right you'll see an example of how it works in the key of D Major, which has two sharps, F# and C#.

D E F# G A B C# D	D Ionian
E F# G A B C# D E	E Dorian
F# G A B C# D E F#	F# Phrygian
G A B C# D E F# G	G Lydian
A B C# D E F# G A	A Mixolydian
B C# D E F# G A B	B Aeolian
C# D E F# G A B C#	C# Locrian

So, now you understand how to name the seven modes of each key, but you're probably asking yourself: How is this really any different from just playing the major scale? Aren't I just playing the same notes in a different order? Why bother naming them something different, won't they just sound the same? Actually, they do sound very different from each other, because the half steps are totally rearranged. You can hear this difference quite clearly if you start each mode on the same root note thereby contrasting them against each other. You will notice immediately how different they are. Try the seven three-note-per-string fingerings below, starting them all on the note C (8th fret of the 6th string). On the CD, you can hear one-octave versions of these modes.

C Ionian

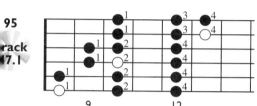

C Dorian

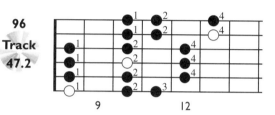

C Phrygian

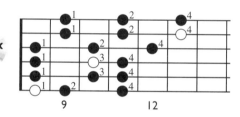

C Lydian

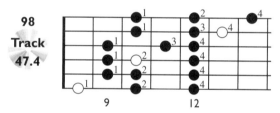

C Mixolydian

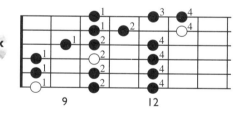

C Aeolian

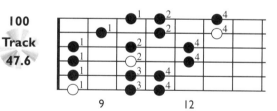

C Locrian

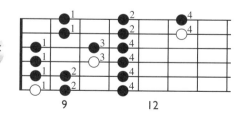

Now that you've learned the names of the modes and a fingering for each one, it's time to learn how to play any mode all over the fretboard using the five major scale forms you learned back on page 51. Here's how it works: Let's pick C# Phrygian as a sample mode to play all over the fretboard.

Step 1) Remember, the Phrygian mode is the third mode, so C# must be the 3rd degree of whatever major key you're in. Backtrack from C# to the root, like so: C#–B–A (3–2–1).

Step 2) Play all five of your A Major scales in the CAGED sequence, but start and end each scale on the note C# instead of the note A. Now you have rearranged the root note to be C# instead of A, so you're playing C#–D–F#–G#–A–B–C# all over the neck. The five C# Phrygian scale forms below are exactly the same as the five major scale forms on page 51, except that the root notes are C# instead of A. You can apply the same principal to every mode, allowing you to play them all over the neck simply by rearranging the root notes in the five major scale forms that you already know.

C# Phrygian (C Form)

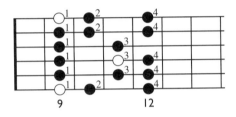

C# Phrygian (E Form)

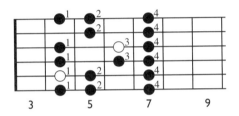

C# Phrygian (A Form)

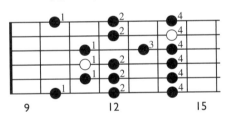

C# Phrygian (D Form)

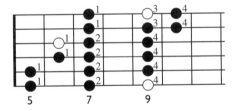

C# Phrygian (G Form)

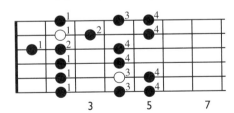

Modal Progressions

A mode can be thought of as a particular series of single notes, as we have discovered in the last section, or as a prevailing *tonality* ("overall sound") expressed by chords, as we're about to discover. The modal choice for improvisation will be determined by the chord progression. So, we must know which group of chords implies which mode.

Just as there are seven different tones in each major key, there are also seven modes and seven chords. Just as the emphasis can be shifted from one root to another in single notes, it can also be shifted in chords. This shifting creates *modal progressions*, progressions in which a chord other than the I chord is the "home chord," around which all the other chords revolve and to which they eventually resolve.

The diatonic triads in all major keys follow this pattern:

I   Major
ii   Minor
iii Minor
IV   Major
V   Major
vi   Minor
vii Diminished

The diatonic 7th chords in all major keys follow the pattern:

I   Major 7th
ii   Minor 7th
iii Minor 7th
IV   Major 7th
V   Dominant 7th
vi   Minor 7th
vii Minor 7th ♭5

(See the Chord Scales chapter on page 48 to review this information.) But, let's get back to the point. To create modal progressions, all we have to do is form them from diatonic chords other than the I chord. If a progression does not include the the I chord, we can choose a different "home chord" for the progression to resolve to. Let's look at an example in the key of A Major to test this theory.

02
ack
8

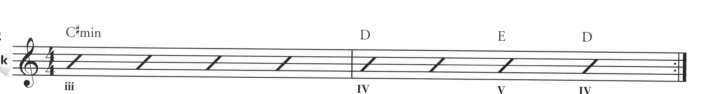

This progression clearly resolves to the iii chord, C♯ Minor. So, its tonality is C♯ Phrygian.

Jefferson Airplane used this type of progression in "White Rabbit."

Now, we'll choose some diatonic chords from the key of G Major. This progression clearly resolves to the chord A Minor, so its tonality is A Dorian. Van Morrison used this kind of progression for "Moondance."

Let's get another Dorian sound, this time, by choosing diatonic 7th chords from the key of F Major. Santana used a progression like this in many hits, including "Evil Ways." This progression has a G Dorian tonality.

Now, we're going to choose diatonic chords from E Major to get a B Mixolydian sound. This type of progression was used by the Grateful Dead in "Fire on the Mountain."

This A Aeolian progression, which can also be called A Minor, has been used in countless rock songs including "Stairway to Heaven," "All Along the Watch Tower" and "Love Song," by The Cure.

Modal Interchange

Modes can be played, not only over chord progressions, but also over *static chords* (chords that are repeated over and over again, instead of progressing to other chords). One way to do this is to match the first mode of a key to the first chord in that key, and the second mode to the second chord, etc. This is rather obvious, but look at the chart to the right to see how it works:

I =	Major triad or major 7th	Play the Ionian mode
ii =	Minor triad or minor 7th	Play the Dorian mode
iii =	Minor triad or minor 7th	Play the Phrygian mode
IV =	Major triad or major 7th	Play the Lydian mode
V =	Major triad or dominant 7th	Play the Mixolydian mode
vi =	Minor triad or minor 7th	Play the Aeolian mode
vii =	Diminished triad or minor 7th♭5	Play the Locrian mode

Another approach involves "faking out" the listener by going for a less obvious, but more exotic mode choice. This is called *modal interchange*. Who is to say whether a static major triad is the I, IV or V chord of a given tonality? Without another chord being present to clarify its position within the key it could really be any of the above. The same is true of a static minor triad.

Is it the ii, the iii or the vi chord? Without another chord being present, it is up to the musician to decide.

The three examples below demonstrate how different modes can be used to solo over a static C Major chord.

So, you have these choices over a major triad: Ionian, Lydian, or Mixolydian modes on the same root.

You have these choices over a minor triad or a minor 7th chord: Dorian, Phrygian or Aeolian modes on the same root.

You have these choices over a major 7th chord: Ionian or Lydian modes on the same root.

If you are soloing over a static chord, it is perfectly fine to switch modes within the same solo, or even the same lick, to create different moods and effects. You can hear Jimi Hendrix touching on this in his unaccompanied solo at Woodstock. Though there are no underlying chords, he implies different modes and chords with his choices of single notes. There is much food for thought and experimentation in this chapter. You should study it in conjunction with the Chord Scales (page 48), Major Scales (page 51) and Theory (page 112) chapters in this book.

Introduction to Slide Guitar

The soulful sounds of slide guitar have been an important part of blues and rock music since the very beginning. Robert Johnson and the other Delta bluesmen were laying the foundations of rock with bottle neck slides way before Jimmy Page, David Gilmour or George Thorogood ever picked them up.

A slide can be a glass bottle that fits over your finger, a piece of metal pipe, a beer bottle, or more or less any object you rub up and down the strings to get a sliding effect. If you can't picture the sound of a slide, just think of the first, slow guitar solo in Lynyrd Skynyrd's "Free Bird," or Duane Allman's solo at the end of "Layla" by Derek and the Dominos.

The picture below shows how a typical metal slide fits over the 4th finger of the left hand. The slide can be put on any finger, but the 4th finger is the most popular choice because it leaves the other three fingers free to play regular chords or scales. This hand-with-slide is properly positioned to begin playing.

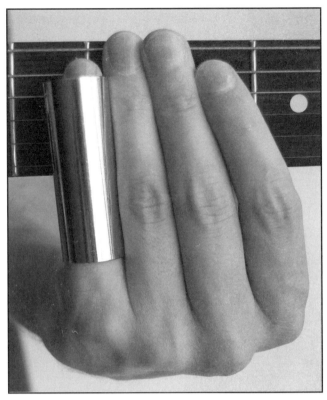

Proper slide position.

When playing slide, it's important to mute behind (to the left of) the slide with one or more of your left-hand fingers. This helps to keep the sound "clean." It's also important to place the slide directly over the metal bar of the fret, not in between the frets. Also, it helps to have a guitar with *high action*. This means that the strings are farther away from the fretboard than usual. If you press too hard with the slide, it will rub against the frets, causing an unpleasant sound. So, high action decreases the chance of this, and makes it easier to play good, clean slide guitar. The exercises that follow are a good introduction to playing slide. Enjoy.

This easy exercise will help you get used to using the slide for the first time. Note that "s" (for "slide") takes the places of the left-hand finger numbers under the TAB staff.

110

Track 51

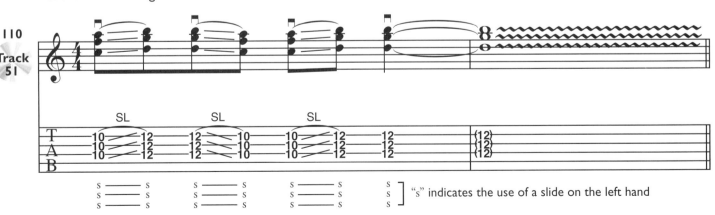

"s" indicates the use of a slide on the left hand

This lick is in the style of George Thorogood's "Bad to the Bone." It's a *call and response* (creating the illusion of two separate guitar parts) between the fingered power chords that begin each phrase and the sliding notes. The slide should be worn on your pinky.

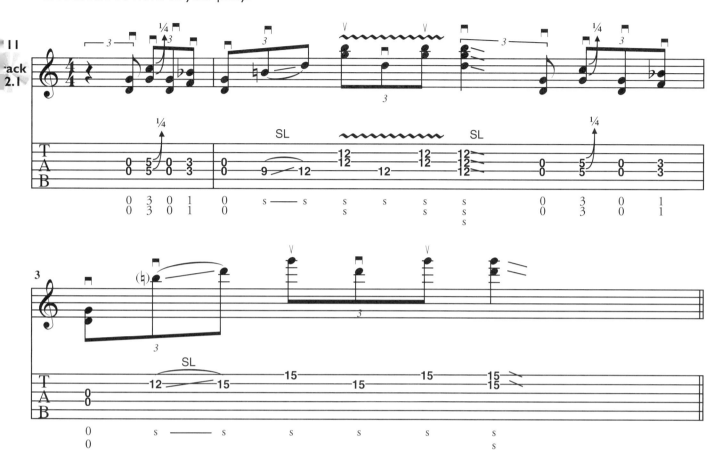

This bluesy slide lick works well over an E7 chord.

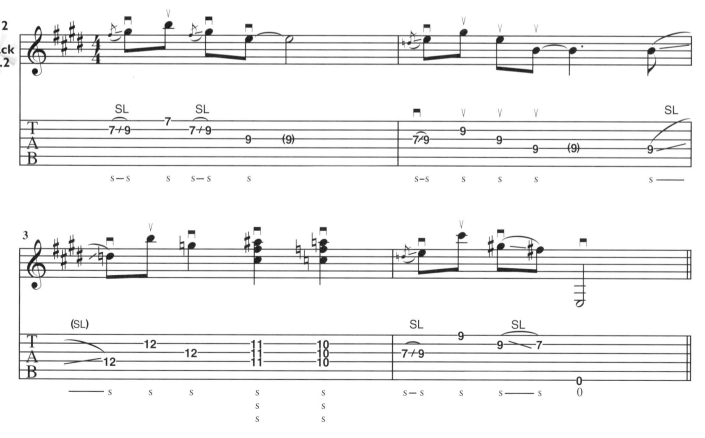

Harmonics

Harmonics are pure, ringing tones that are produced by picking the string while gently touching it at various points along its length. In most cases, the finger should touch the string directly above the fret. As soon as the harmonic is picked, the finger should be removed so that the string can vibrate freely, without interference. The root, 3rd, 5th and 9th of any string can be produced easily with *natural harmonics* (harmonics of the open strings). The best spots to get harmonics are the 12th, 7th, 5th, 19th and 24th frets. We'll also be learning to produce them at other frets and slightly to the left or right of certain frets.

All guitars are not created equally when it comes to harmonic response. Some work much more easily than others. Fresh strings help on any guitar, as does picking close to the bridge. Whether you're using your fingers or a pick, attacking the strings about ¾'s of an inch from the bridge will make any harmonic ring more loudly and clearly. Also, on electric guitars the bridge pickup usually works best, and high gain distortion may enhance certain harmonics, or create harmonic "sweet spots" where none previously existed. A freshly strung acoustic steel-string guitar produces a wide array of beautiful harmonics.

Playing a harmonic:

1. Touch the 6th string directly above the 12th fret with your left-hand 1st finger.

2. Pick the 6th string.

3. Remove the left-hand finger immediately.

◇ = Harmonic

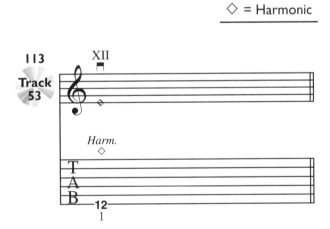

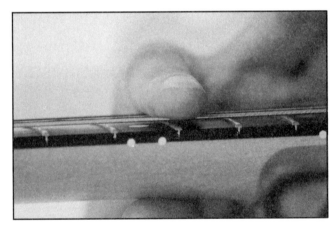

Playing a harmonic.

The following fretboard chart shows the note names of the easiest natural harmonics. Harmonics played at these frets are by far the most common in all forms of guitar music.

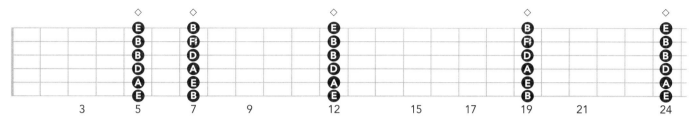

This exercise will get you started playing harmonics on the frets in the chart above. The Roman numerals indicate at which fret to play the harmonic. If you don't have 24 frets on your guitar, you can still get those harmonics by placing your finger where the 24th fret would be if you had one.

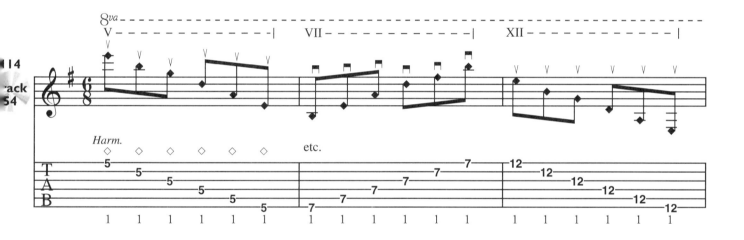

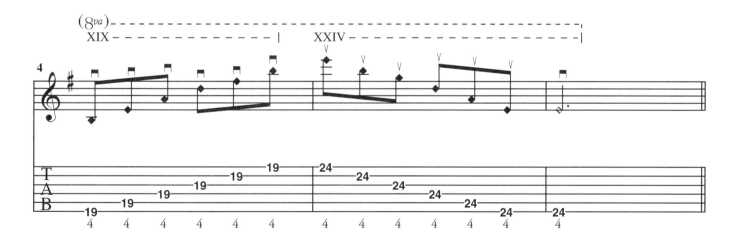

This short, meditative *etude,* or study, is entirely composed of natural harmonics formed on the 5th, 7th and 12th frets. It's important to let each note ring as long as possible to get the most musical effect.

Midnight Wind Song

Artificial Harmonics

Artificial harmonics are usually produced using fretted notes rather than open strings. Any of the 12 tones can be played with a number of different artificial harmonic techniques, all of which have unique sounds. This gives both the electric and the acoustic guitar quite a bit of versatility and sonic flare. In rock, the most commonly used artificial harmonic technique is called the *pinch harmonic*. This produces the screaming harmonic wail that is usually attached to a string bend in the style of Billy Gibbons of ZZ Top or Eddie Van Halen and Zakk Wylde. *Tapped harmonics* and *harp harmonics* are also used sometimes, creating different effects. In this section, we'll be learning the above-mentioned techniques, and applying them in rock licks.

Playing a Pinch Harmonic

1. Fret the 5th string, 2nd-fret B note with your left hand.

2. Locate the spot on the same string where the 26th fret would be if you had one.

3. Pick the spot with a downstroke of the pick and allow the string to snap back and touch your thumb at exactly that spot on the string.

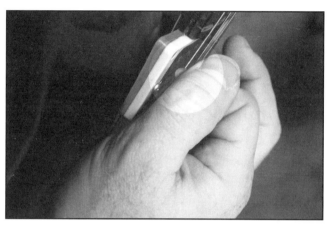

Playing a pinch harmonic.

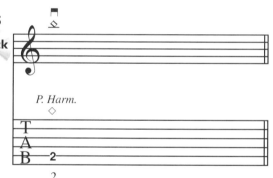

Note: The spot at which you pick to produce the harmonic is called a *sweet spot*. There are several strong sweet spots on each string between the end of the neck and the bridge. These spots change as the fretted note changes and differ slightly from guitar to guitar. You'll have to get to know your guitar and where the sweet spots for certain frets align with "landmarks" like your pickup's pole pieces, the end of your fretboard, the screws in your pickguard, etc.

Playing a Tapped Harmonic

1. Fret the G note on the low-E string 3rd fret with your 1st finger.

2. Use your right-hand index finger to sharply tap the same string directly above the 15th fret.

3. Remove the tapping finger quickly, so that it doesn't mute the string.

Note: Tapping exactly 12 frets above any note will produce a harmonic pitch one octave above the fretted note. The fretted note and the octave harmonic will blend equally. Van Halen used this technique to begin his unaccompanied acoustic solo, "Spanish Fly."

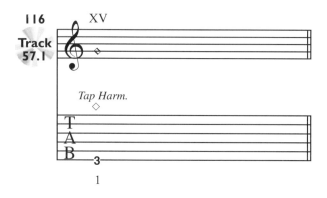

Playing a Harp Harmonic

1. Finger the 3rd fret C note on the 5th string.

2. Lightly touch the same string with your right-hand index finger on the 15th fret. This finger must be positioned exactly above the fret wire.

3. With the other two fingers still in place, use your right thumb to pluck the string between the higher fret and the bridge. (The string can also be plucked with a pick held between the thumb and 2nd finger.)

4. Remove the right hand as soon as the note has been plucked so that it doesn't mute the string.

Note: The resulting harmonic will be one octave higher than the fretted note.

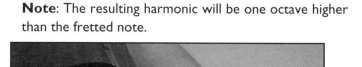

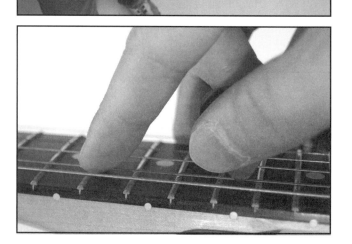

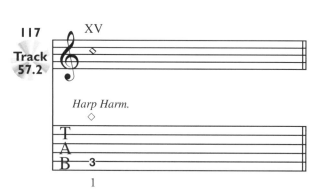

You may have noticed that the pinch harmonic, tapped harmonic and harp harmonic techniques are all based on the practice of going 12 frets higher than a fretted note to produce a harmonic that is one octave higher in pitch. Using the harmonic techniques mentioned above—at distances other than 12 frets higher than the fretted note—yields different harmonic tones. The following formulas hold true for all artificial harmonic techniques.

4 frets above the fundamental	=	Artificial harmonic a major 3rd + two octaves above the fundamental
5 frets above the fundamental	=	Artificial harmonic two octaves above the fundamental
7 frets above the fundamental	=	Artificial harmonic a 5th + an octave above the fundamental
12 frets above the fundamental	=	Artificial harmonic one octave above the fundamental
16 frets above the fundamental	=	Artificial harmonic a major 3rd + two octaves above the fundamental
19 frets above the fundamental	=	Artificial harmonic a 5th + an octave above the fundamental
24 frets above the fundamental	=	Artificial harmonic two octaves above the fundamental

This tapped harmonic riff uses the above concept to create a cool effect. Hear the harmonic change as you tap on different frets, even though your left hand stays in the same location.

Pick slide = Scrape the side of your pick along the string

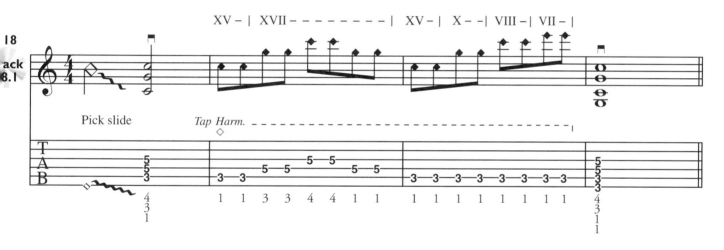

This G Minor lick has some *pinch harmonic bends*. For this technique, use the pinch harmonic technique you learned on page 85 on a note that you are bending.

Dude Etudes and Lilith Licks

It's time to forget the scales and theory and play some music. Both the "Dude Etudes" and "Lilith Licks" sound very musical and combine many of the techniques and styles we've covered so far. They also function as *duets*.

Lilith Licks 1 and 2, when played simultaneously, comprise "The Turquoise Duet."

Track 59 *The Turquoise Duet*

Dude Etudes 1 and 2, when combined, make up "The Metallic Duet."

Track 60 *The Metallic Duet*

PHOTO BY EDWARD G. LINES, JR./COURTESY OF STAR FILE PHOTO, INC.

Tom Morello (b. 1964) is best known as guitarist for the bands Rage Against the Machine and Audioslave. With these bands, he helped create a pioneering blend of heavy metal, hip-hop and funk. His guitar style is notable for quick hammer-ons and pull-offs, creative use of effects and use of a kill switch to mimic the sound of a DJ.

Lilith Lick 1

Track
61

Lilith Lick 2

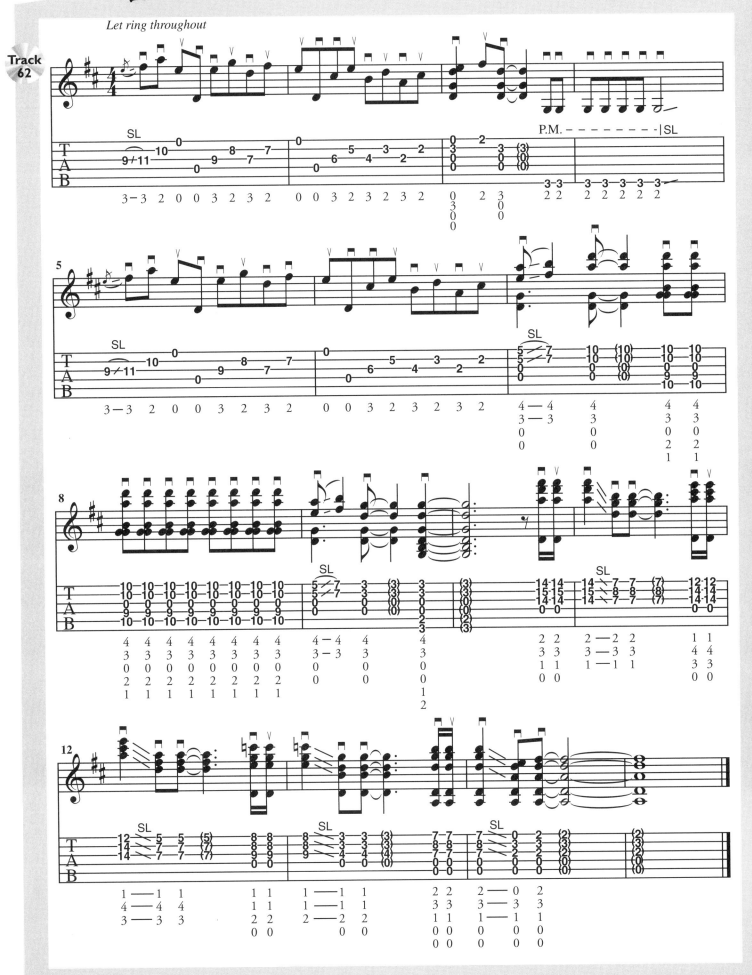

Dude Etude 1

Dude Etude 2

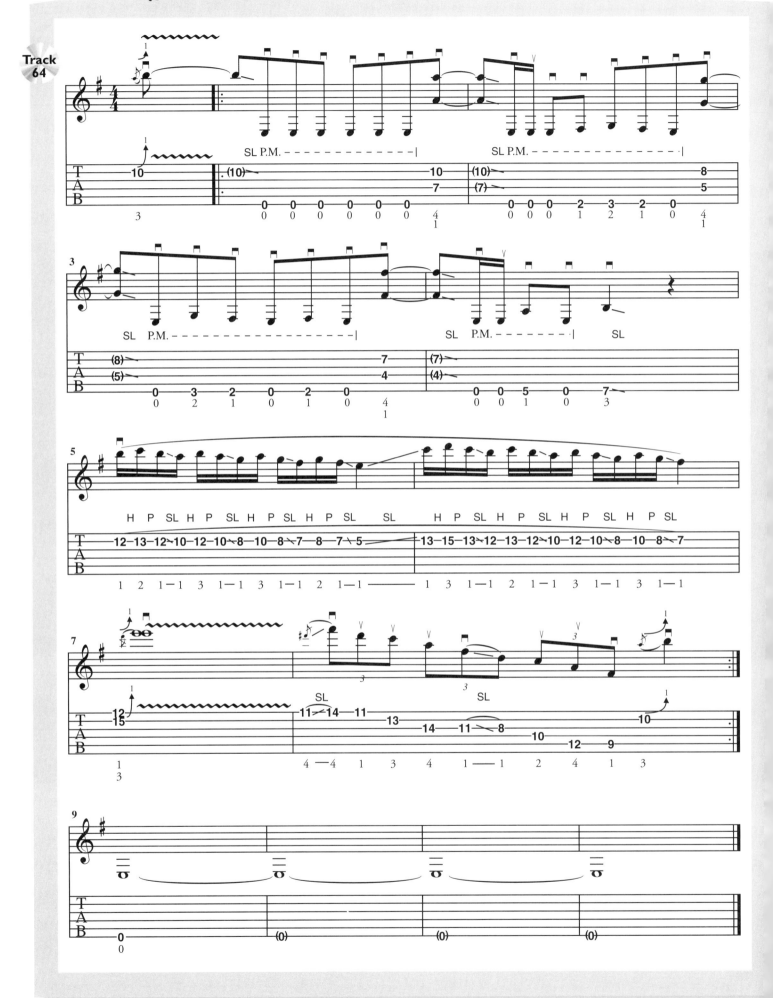

Improv (Phrasing)

Once a decent amount of technique and some "ammunition" such as scales, chords, licks, theory and arpeggios have been learned by the guitarist, questions may still remain. What do I do with all of this stuff? Why does it sound like gibberish when *I* play a solo, but it totally rules when David Gilmour plays one? Why can I play really fast, but it just doesn't sound very musical? Do any of these concerns sound familiar?

The solution to your problem lies in *phrasing*. Phrasing in music is analogous to punctuation in writing. What if you were to read this paragraph aloud, but you never paused when there was a comma or a period, and you never changed the tone of your voice when asking a question, and you never emphasized any words to help make your point? What if you also slurred your words and mispronounced several others? If you read aloud in this manner, you wouldn't be communicating very well and the experience may be unpleasant for both you and the listener. If you played guitar without attention to clear articulation, normal pausing, accents and inflections, that wouldn't be enjoyable either.

A good way to approach soloing is much like normal speaking: Accurately execute some distinct ideas that are separated by spaces, so that one idea can be differentiated from another. Listen to the solo from "Another Brick in the Wall, Part II" by Pink Floyd. Each musical phrase is separated by a distinct gap of silence. Some of the gaps are quite long causing anticipation before the next lick. This is very effective. It's also good to repeat the same idea several times with slight variations. This gets the listener familiar with a theme, but still interested in what will happen next. You can also try building intensity during your solo, gradually subsiding, and then rebuilding it for a climax. Jimmy Page's solo in "Stairway to Heaven" uses this technique, and is widely acclaimed as one of the greatest rock guitar solos of all time.

Trading Licks with Yourself

Check out the A Minor Jam backing track (page 95, CD track 66). Just listen to it without playing, for now. Try to imagine the sound of two guitarists trading licks of the same length (two bars each) over the backing track. You'll probably have to tap your foot and count along to "feel" how long each lick should last. The first guitarist only knows how to play slow bluesy bends. The other guitarist only plays scale passages. Now, begin playing in the A Minor scale, which matches that track. First you play two bars of slow bends, then two bars of scales. Either sustain a note toward the end of each phrase, or leave a complete gap between licks. This is a great introduction to phrasing. If you haven't tried it before, you'll find yourself playing in a whole new style!

Variation: Allow yourself to play anything you want, but keep the two-bar lick trading structure.

Listen to Eddie Van Halen's solo on "You Really Got Me." Count it out. You'll notice that it fits this structure, as does his solo in "Panama" and much of his other work.

The 2nd Ending

The *2nd ending* is a phrasing technique in which a lick is played, and then repeated, but with a different ending.

You can keep on going with more and more endings as long as you like. The following is an example of this in A Minor. Try it over the A Minor Jam backing track (page 95, CD track 66). Then, keep improvising with the same technique.

Phrasing is a topic to which an entire book could be devoted. My advice is to work on what you've learned so far, but also to listen a lot to your favorite players and try to analyze their unique phrasing styles. Then add some of that into your own style. Good luck!

Backing Tracks

The backing tracks on the CD are very useful for practicing the licks and scales you've been learning in this book.

Backing Track 1

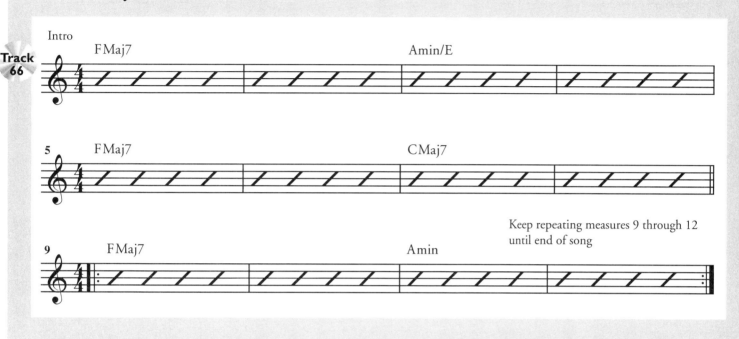

A Minor Jam

Track 66

Intro | FMaj7 | Amin/E

5 | FMaj7 | CMaj7

Keep repeating measures 9 through 12 until end of song

9 | FMaj7 | Amin

Backing Track 2

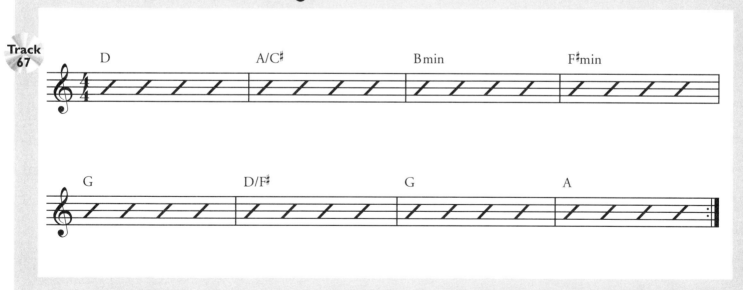

Ballad in D Major

Track 67

D | A/C♯ | Bmin | F♯min

G | D/F♯ | G | A

Backing Track 3

Blues in E

Track 68

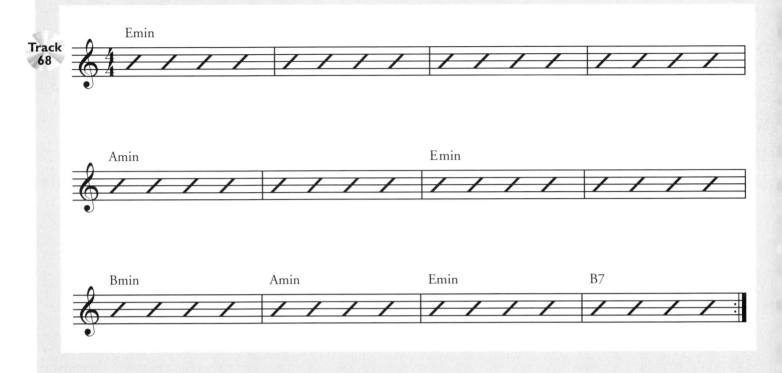

Backing Track 4

B Minor Jam

Track 69

Repeat measures 5 through 8 until the end of the song

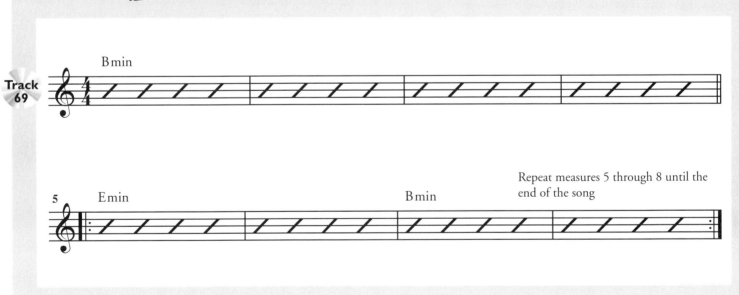

Single-String Licks

Many guitarists approach melodies, licks and lead guitar by moving from string to string in a single *position* (a span of four consecutive frets). "Position playing" is very useful, but after a while the player may feel "trapped," or "boxed in." Then it's time to "break out of the box," and move from left to right on the same string. This enables easy motion up or down the neck, and also encourages an expanded melodic vocabulary. The exercises that follow are all designed to help build this *position shifting* ability. They're also good vehicles for developing single-string skills.

This sliding exercise covers all of the natural notes (notes that are not sharp or flat) on the 1st string.

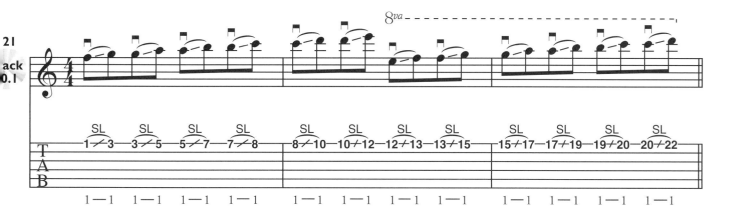

The exercise below combines hammer-ons, pull-offs and slides, and climbs up and down the natural notes of the G string.

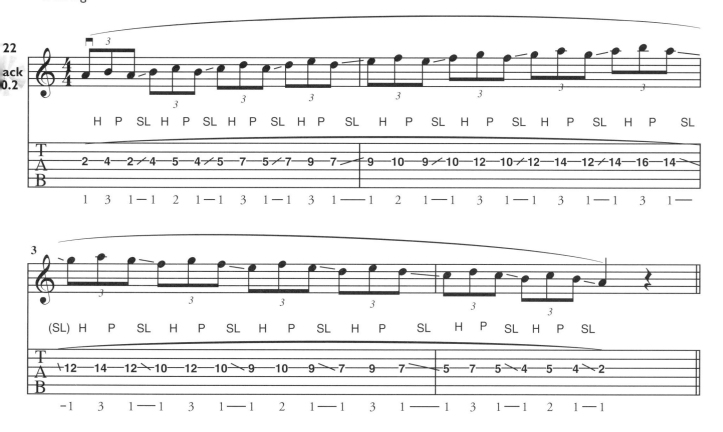

This "sixes sequence" in C Major climbs up and down the
B string. It's a great chops builder and can be used as a
speed picking drill. Notice it's the 1st finger that always
moves the sequence higher or lower on the string.

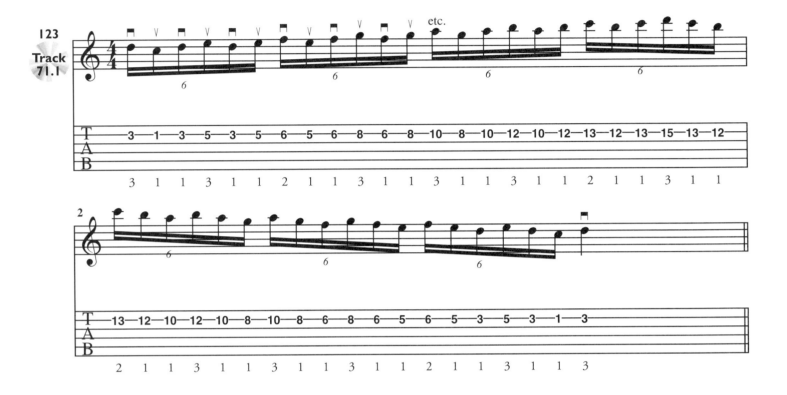

This single-string lick is in the style of Blink 182's
"Carousel." It can be called the "punk pull-off" because
it's found in so many hardcore songs.

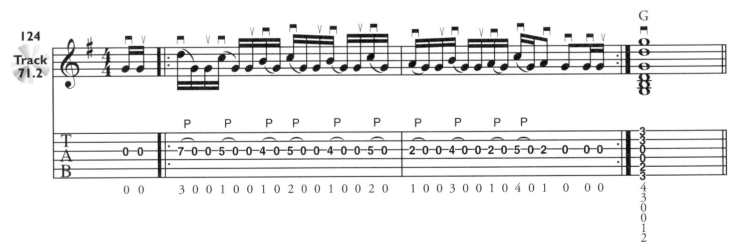

The Art of Finger Tapping

Prog rock pioneer Steve Hackett of Genesis was *finger tapping* way back in the early 1970s, but Eddie Van Halen went on to develop and popularize the technique in 1978 with the ground-breaking self-titled release, *Van Halen*. Soon everyone in heavy metal had jumped on the tapping band wagon and the science evolved to undreamed of levels of proficiency, the highest of which was probably achieved by jazz chops monger, Stanley Jordan, with his piano-like "magic touch."

Finger tapping is the act of hammering-on with a right-hand finger or fingers in addition to the left hand. It's very easy to get started, and facilitates lightning fast, fluid passages with wide interval leaps.

This easy example is in the style of Van Halen's signature "Eruption" lick. The motion is: Tap–Pull–Hammer, again and again. Try it over an A Minor chord.

T = *Tap* the note with a right-hand finger

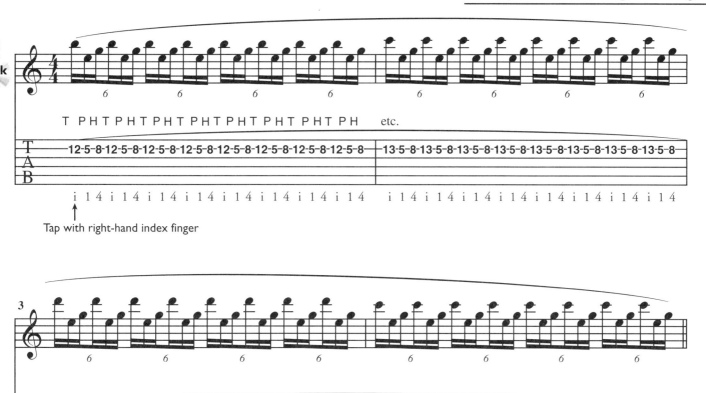

Tap with right-hand index finger

This example doubles the tapped note like Randy Rhoads did in the "Crazy Train" solo. Try it over an A Major chord.

This example links two string-skipping, multi-tapped arpeggios together, D and A Major. (We have entered the shred zone.)

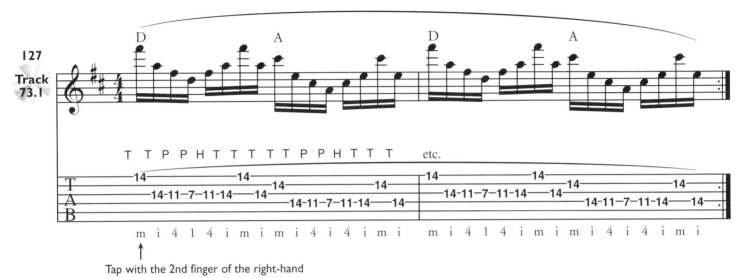

Tap with the 2nd finger of the right-hand

This example creates a *pedal tone* effect, in which the E note is repeated throughout an E Minor scale passage.

In this Van Halen-style lick, the *quintuplet* rhythm (five-notes-per-beat; see Tuplets, page 126) and the use of open strings make for an interesting sound. Try it over an A Minor chord.

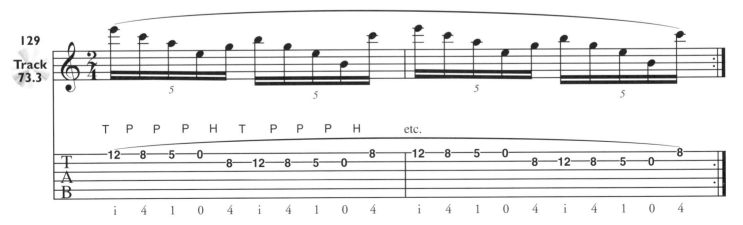

The following example introduces a new rhythm that divides each beat into nine notes of equal value. This can be called the *triple triplet*. This example consists of an E Major 7th arpeggio.

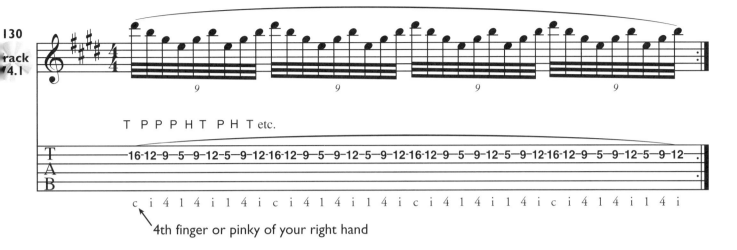

4th finger or pinky of your right hand

This example expands on the previous idea by adding another finger on the right hand; that's three right-hand fingers. The extra finger adds the 13th, making it an E Major 13th arpeggio.

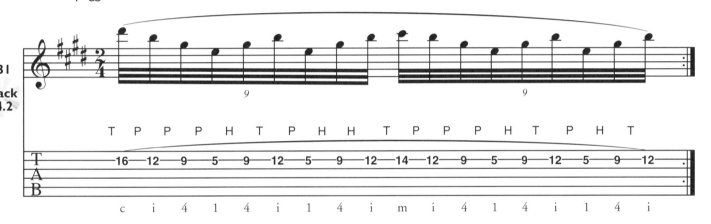

This is another method of playing an arpeggio with string-skipping, multi-finger tapping. It's a D Major arpeggio.

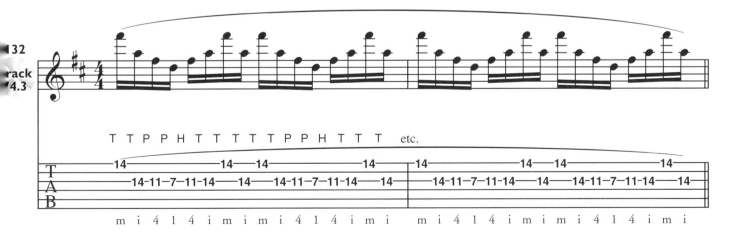

Now you are ready for a full-length piece using finger tapping. This is based on the chord changes in Pachelbel's *Canon in D Major*.

Tapping the Canon

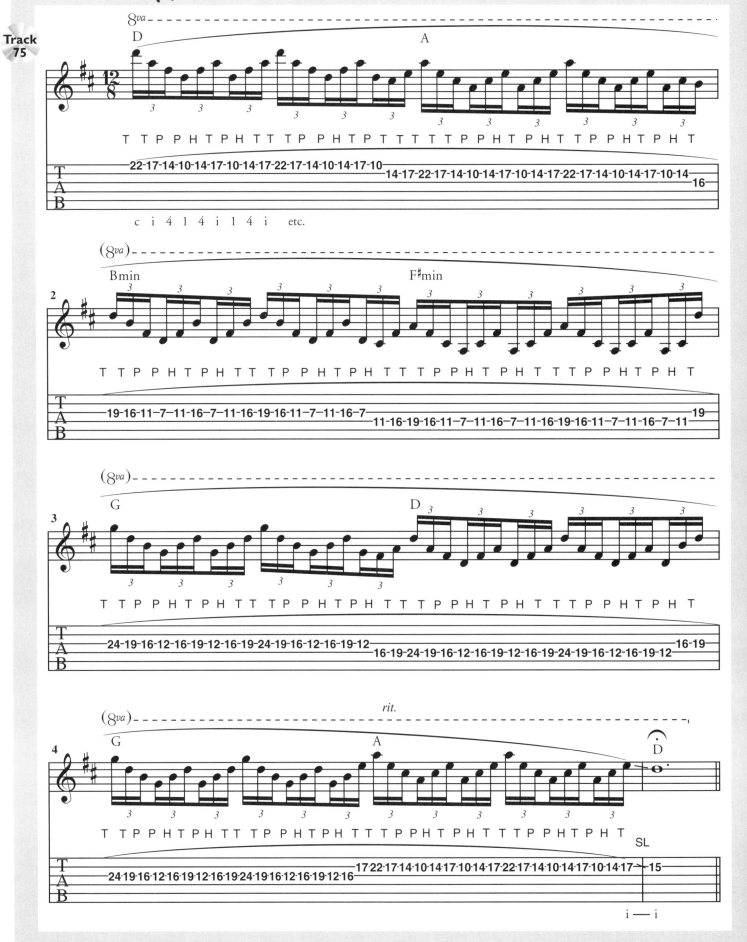

The Art of the Sweep Arpeggio

In Italian, the word *arpeggio* means "broken chord." As you learned on page 20, to play an arpeggio is to play the notes in a chord one at a time. Sometimes an arpeggio is played by fingering a chord and plucking a series of notes within that chord, so that each note rings together (for examples of this, see page 46). However, arpeggios can also be played with separated notes that do not ring together. Some techniques used for doing this include finger tapping, sweep picking and alternate picking. This chapter is all about sweep-picked arpeggios. By studying the chord construction section of the theory appendix (page 115), you'll be able to spell out the notes in any chord or arpeggio.

Sweep-picked arpeggios almost always have only one note per string. The idea is to use a series of consecutive downstrokes of the pick to ascend through the arpeggio tones, and to then use a series of consecutive upstrokes to descend back down the arpeggio. You should use one fluid and continuous pick stroke that glides down and up the strings as if you were slowly strumming a chord form. Do not separately define each stroke as if you were alternate picking a scale. Each arpeggio you're about to learn is part of a coordinated system which will allow you to play any major or minor arpeggio in root position, 1st inversion or 2nd inversion (see page 119).

This 1st inversion E Major arpeggio form is a great way to get started sweep picking across all of the strings.

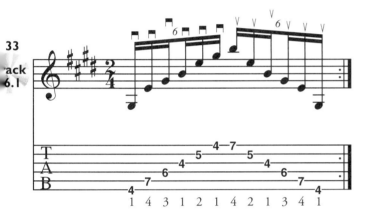

This is the root position E Major arpeggio form.

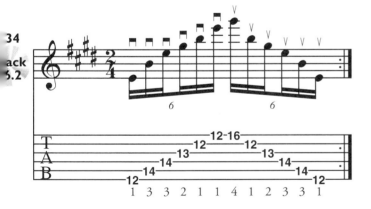

The mastery of sweep arpeggios is very challenging. They must be practiced slowly with perfect technique before they can be accurately sped up. The use of a *metronome* (a device that provides a steady beat) to ensure slow, steady practice and gradual, controlled increase of tempo is highly recommended.

This is the 2nd inversion E Major arpeggio form.

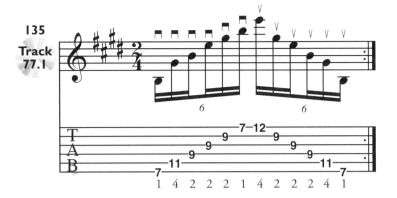

This is the root position E Minor arpeggio form.

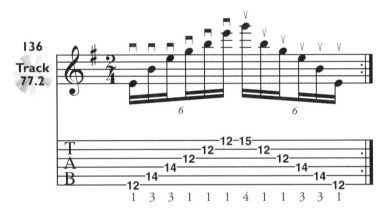

This is the 1st inversion E Minor arpeggio form.

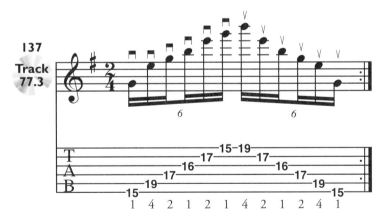

This is the 2nd inversion E Minor arpeggio form.

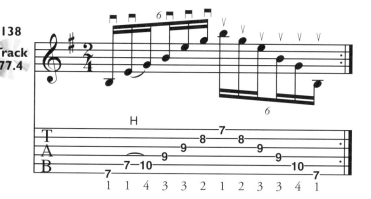

Now that you've learned the inversions of the major and minor arpeggios, we're going to practice connecting them with slides. This will enable you to follow chord progressions with arpeggio forms and also improvise cool licks in your solos.

This exercise connects the inversions of the G Major arpeggio straight up the neck. The first note of each slide is picked with an upstroke.

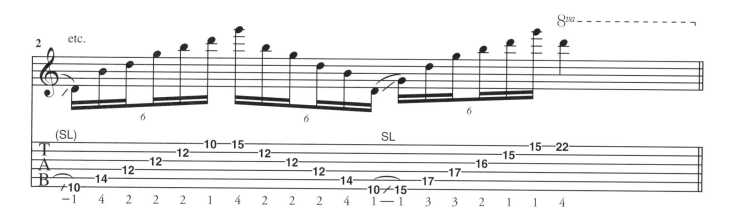

This exercise connects the inversions of the G Minor arpeggio straight up the neck. The first note of each slide is picked with an upstroke.

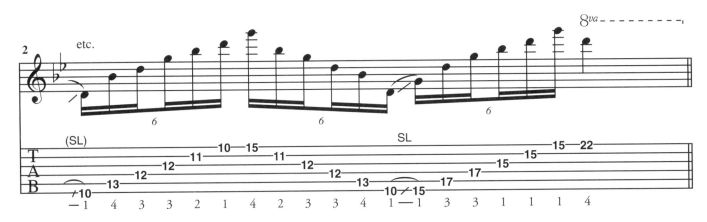

Steve Vai (b. 1960) is an influential virtuoso guitarist. As a teenager, he studied with Joe Satriani, and then went on to attend the Berklee College of Music. His impressive transcription and sight-reading skills earned him a gig with Frank Zappa's band. He gained a wider audience in the mid-80s as a member of David Lee Roth's group. Vai's playing is characterized by technical facility and deep knowledge of music theory, and he played a large role in popularizing the 7-string guitar. He tours with his own group and with Joe Satriani as part of G3.

This etude shows you how to sweep arpeggios over a popular chord progression.

Sweeping the Hotel

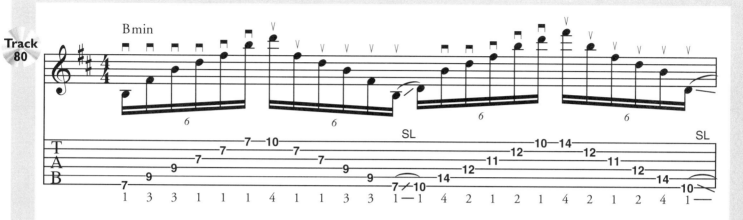

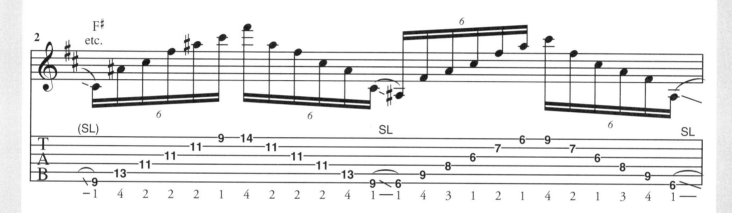

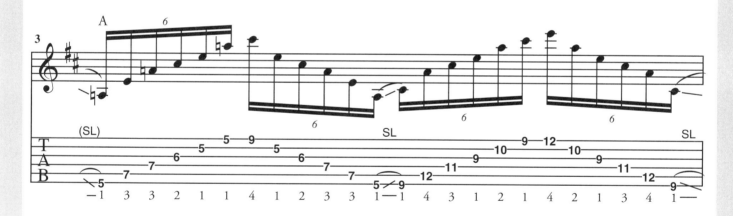

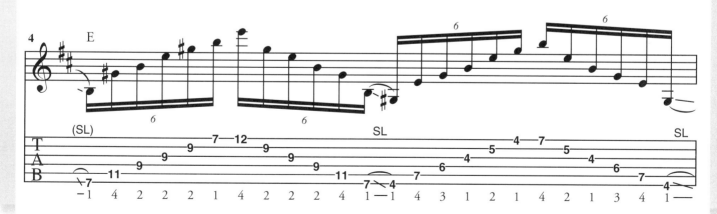

Continued on page 108

Continued from page 107

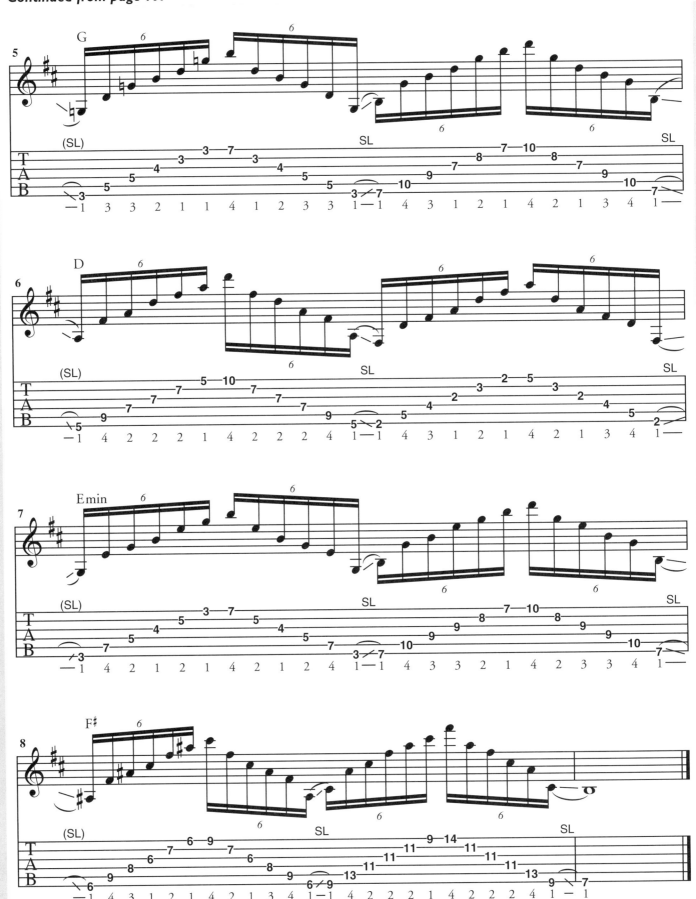

The Art of Speed Picking

The trick to mastering speed picking is to choose some very simple patterns and practice alternate picking them tirelessly, until they get really fast (see pages 22–24 for a review of picking logic). Then learn how to connect these simple patterns, which we will call *scale fragments*, into longer runs. Getting lightning fast at any technique requires the discipline to play slowly at first. The harder you concentrate on the opposite of your goal, which is playing slowly, the sooner you will actually reach your goal, which is playing fast. So, dust off your metronome and get ready to rock! Each exercise must be played at a snail's pace, with perfect accuracy before you begin the process of gradually speeding up.

C Major Scale Fragment 1

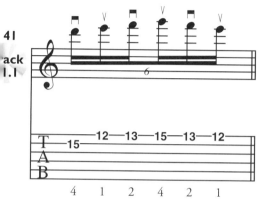

C Major Scale Fragment 2

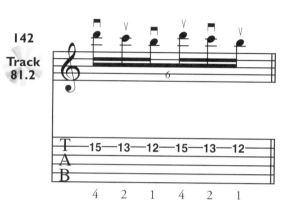

C Major Scale Fragment 3

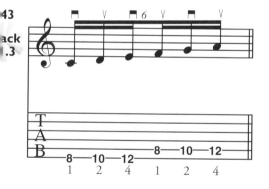

C Major Scale Fragment 4

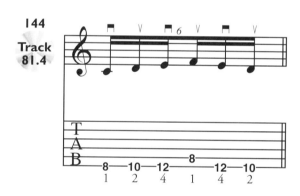

C Major Scale Fragment 5

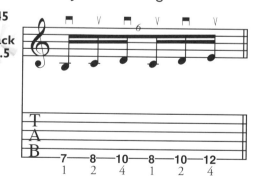

C Major Scale Fragment 6

Now that you have some fragments to work with, we'll begin assembling them into longer runs. Check out this A Minor scale sequence.

147
Track 82

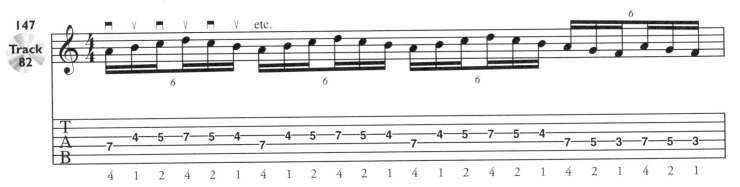

Jennifer Batten is an extremely versatile guitarist who rose from the underground to command her peers' attention. Her big break came in 1987, when she was selected from a pool of 100 guitarists to join Michael Jackson's touring band. She has also played with Jeff Beck, Natalie Cole, The Immigrants and Sara Hickman. She did a feature in Hot Guitarist's video magazine and is now recording her third solo CD.

PHOTO COURTESY OF JENNIFER BATTEN

This scorching lick combines Fragments 1 and 2 and spans more than two octaves of the D Dorian mode. Remember, if we are focusing on the D note—but using the notes belonging to the C Major scale—we are using the D Dorian mode; see pages 74–75 for more on the Dorian mode.

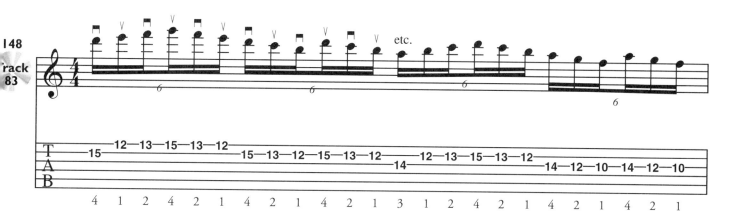

2

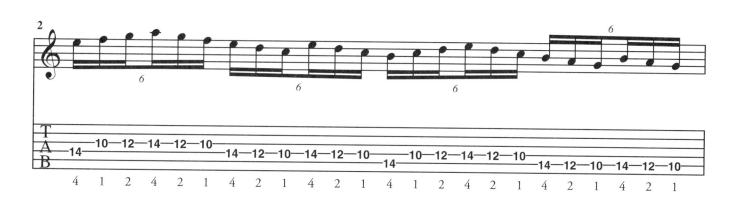

3

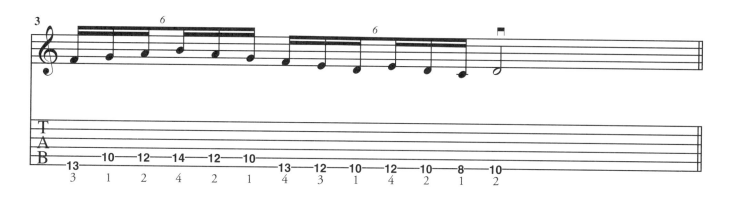

PART 4: Appendix

An Introduction to Music Theory

Most aspects of music theory involve the manipulation or alteration of notes found in the common major scale. Therefore, learning about the major scale is a good first step in the study of music theory.

The Major Scale and Key

The *major scale* is a series of seven different notes separated by the following intervals:

W	= Whole step
H	= Half step

W   W   H   W   W   W   H

This scale is familiar to many of us as the do–re–mi–fa–sol–la–ti–do scale. Here is an example of the major scale, starting on the note C.

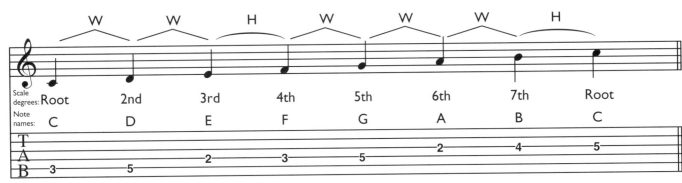

This formula will work starting on any note. The note you start on becomes the *tonic*, or *root*, of the scale. The C Major scale is the only major scale that contains no sharps or flats. Following the formula of whole steps and half steps for the major scale starting on any other root will require the use of either sharps or flats. No major scale has both sharps and flats; it's either a sharp key or a flat key. Try it starting on G. You will find that the 7th note must be changed from F to F♯ to stay with the formula.

Key

A *key* consists of all the notes of a particular scale and takes its name from the root note of that scale. For instance, the notes in the C Major scale above make up the *key of C*.

Minor Key

Every major key has a *relative minor key*. If you count up to the 6th degree of the major scale, you will find the root note of its relative minor key. For instance, the relative minor of C Major is A Minor (C = 1, D = 2, E = 3, F = 4, G = 5, A = 6). If you play a C Major scale, but start and end on A, you will get the A Minor scale.

Key Signatures

The *key signature* appears after the clef at the beginning of every line of music. It tells us the key of the song. It consists of the sharps and flats that result from building a major or minor scale on the root note of the key. For instance, the key of G contains only one sharp, F♯. The key signature for G Major, then, is an F♯. Each key has its own unique combination of sharps or flats. Study the chart below. It shows the key signatures for all the major and minor keys (except C Major and A Minor, which have no sharps or flats in the key signature).

SHARP KEYS

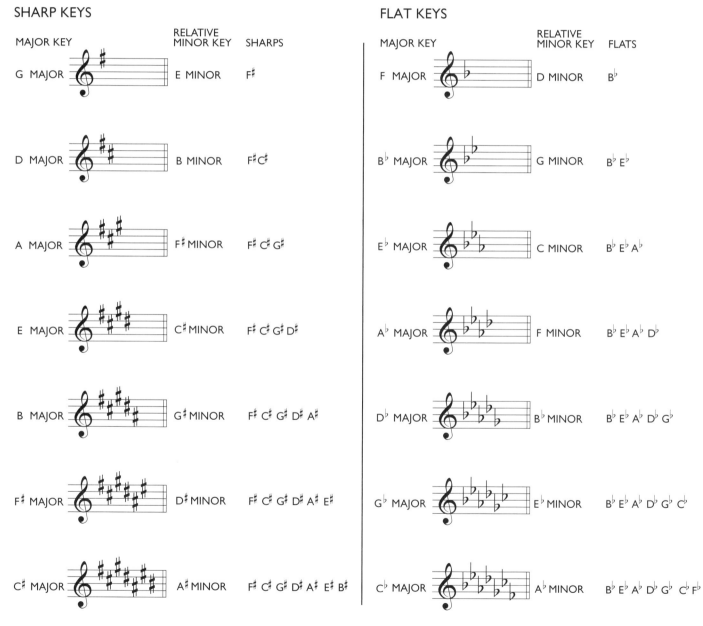

FLAT KEYS

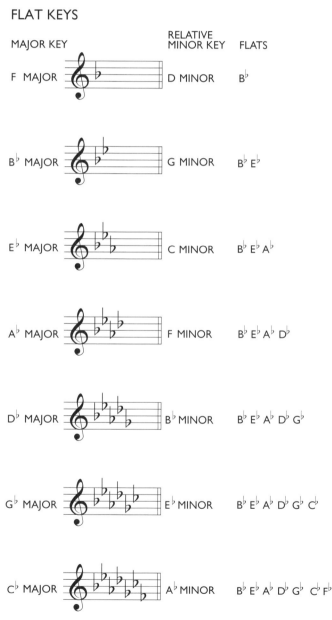

Cycle of 5ths

The *cycle of 5ths* depicts all 15 keys in a logical sequence. When viewed as a clockwise progression, each key is a perfect 5th above the last. When viewed as a counter-clockwise progression, each key is a perfect 4th above the last. C Major is the only key with no accidentals (sharps or flats). The rest of the cycle is divided into two sides, the right side containing keys with sharps and the left containing keys with flats. Moving clockwise away from C, each scale will have one more sharp than the last until C♯ has been reached, in which all seven notes are sharp. Moving counter clockwise away from C each scale will have one more flat than the last until C♭ is reached, in which all seven notes are flat.

To use the cycle of fifths to determine which notes are sharp in a major scale you must know the order of sharps: F♯, C♯, G♯, D♯, A♯, E♯ and B♯. This order of sharps starts directly to the right of the key of C and continues for six clockwise steps in the cycle (through the keys of G, D, A, E, B and F♯). For instance, the A Major scale has three sharps. These three sharps will be the first three in the order of sharps: F♯, C♯ and G♯. The G Major scale has one sharp. That sharp is the first in the order of sharps: F♯. All of the other sharp keys work in the same fashion.

The order of flats is the reverse of the order of sharps, B♭, E♭, A♭, D♭, G♭, C♭ and F♭. The flats function in the same way. The key of B♭ has two flats. They are the first two in the order of flats: B♭ and E♭. The key of A♭ has four flats. They are B♭, E♭, A♭ and D♭.

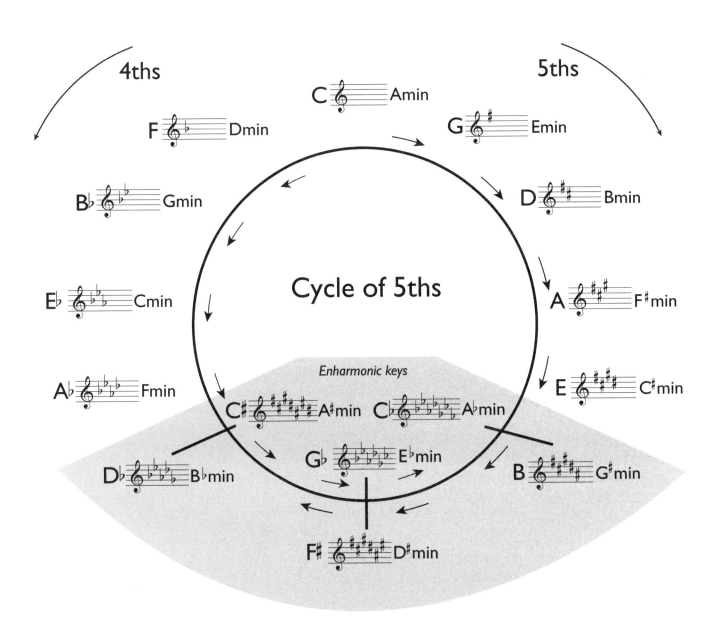

The keys at the bottom of the cycle of 5ths diagram on page 114 are called *enharmonic equivalents*. Enharmonic notes sound the same but can be spelled in two different ways. For instance, C♯ and D♭ are found on the same fret, and sound the same, even though they have different names. C♯ and D♭ are enharmonic equivalents. The three pairs of enharmonic scales shown in the cycle of 5ths are fingered in the same way and sound identical, but are spelled differently. The addition of the three extra scales, that are generated through enharmonics, changes the total number of scales from 12 to 15. This allows the cycle to fit together more neatly.

How Chords Are Derived from the Major Scale

A *chord* is any three or more notes played together. The most basic kind of chord is a *triad*. Triads are built by stacking notes from a scale in *3rds*. By 3rd, we mean that the total distance between these notes encompasses three notes. For instance, from C to E is a 3rd (C = 1, D = 2, E = 3). From E to G is a 3rd (E = 1, F = 2, G = 3). We can start on any scale tone and skip every other note to stack 3rds.

We can build any chord with simple number formulas if we assign every note in the major scale a number, 1 through 7. For instance, the formula for a major triad is 1 3 5. The chart below shows how to build an A Major triad by stacking 3rds from the A Major scale.

The major triad formula =	1		3		5			
The A Major scale = A	B	C♯	D	E	F♯	G♯	A	
1	2	3	4	5	6	7	8 (1)	
The A Major triad = A		C♯		E				
1 ╲3rd╱	3	╲3rd╱	5					

Often, chord tones are *altered* (made sharp or flat) to create different chord types. The chart below demonstrates how an E Minor 7th chord (Emin7) is derived from the E Major scale using this number system by stacking 3rds and changing the 3 to ♭3 and the 7 to ♭7.

The minor 7 formula =	1		♭3		5		♭7		
The E Major scale =	E	F♯	G♯	A	B	C♯	D♯	E	
	1	2	3	4	5	6	7	8 (1)	
The Emin7 chord =	E		G		B		D		
	1		♭3		5		♭7		

└──── Changes ────┘

Here is a reference chart of important chord formulas. You should learn those that you don't know. Get a good chord encyclopedia, such as the *Guitar Chord Encyclopedia* (Alfred #4432), and learn fingerings for all of them.

Table of Chord Formulas

Type	* Symbol with C Root	Formula
Major triad	C	1 – 3 – 5
Minor triad	Cmin	1 – ♭3 – 5
Diminished triad	Cdim	1 – ♭3 – ♭5
Augmented triad	Caug	1 – 3 – ♯5
Major 7th	CMaj7	1 – 3 – 5 – 7
Minor 7th	Cmin7	1 – ♭3 – 5 – ♭7
Dominant 7th	C7	1 – 3 – 5 – ♭7
Diminished 7th	Cdim7	1 – ♭3 – ♭5 – ♭♭7**
Minor 7th ♭5	Cmin7♭5	1 – ♭3 – ♭5 – ♭7
Minor/Major 7	Cmin/Maj7	1 – ♭3 – 5 – 7
Dominant 7th ♭9	C7♭9	1 – 3 – 5 – ♭7 – ♭9
Dominant 7th ♯9	C7♯9	1 – 3 – 5 – ♭7 – ♯9
Dominant 7th ♭5	C7♭5	1 – 3 – ♭5 – ♭7
Dominant 7th ♯5	C7♯5	1 – 3 – ♯5 – ♭7
Major add 9	Cadd9	1 – 3 – 5 – 9
Minor add 9	Cmin add9	1 – ♭3 – 5 – 9
Major 6	C6	1 – 3 – 5 – 6
Minor 6	Cmin6	1 – ♭3 – 5 – 6
Suspended 4th	Csus4	1 – 4 – 5
Suspended 2nd	Csus2	1 – 2 – 5
Dominant 7th suspended 4th	C7sus4	1 – 4 – 5 – ♭7

* The term *symbol* refers to how a chord name is written in a piece of music.

** ♭♭ = *Double flat* lowers the note two half steps.

Chord Extensions and Alterations

All of the numbers in these chord names reflect the number system covered on page 115. One of these numbers, 9, appears not to be from the seven numbers generated by the major scale. Numbers higher than 8 are called *extensions*. These numbers are easily generated by writing a two-octave major scale and applying the number system. Using the chart to the right you can easily observe that a CMaj add9 chord is a CMaj triad with a D added above.

Two-Octave C Scale with Extensions

								Extensions						
C	D	E	F	G	A	B	C	D	E	F	G	A	B	C
1	2	3	4	5	6	7	8	9	10	11	12	13	14	15

Extensions such as 13ths, 9ths and 11ths can be added to major 7th, minor 7th or dominant 7th chords merely by adding the appropriate note to the 7th chord. The addition of tones such as the 13th imply the presence of sequential chord tones such as the 9th and 11th, though these tones are often omitted. Certain chord tones, such as 5 and 9, are sometimes altered (sharped or flatted). *Double alterations* such as the 7♯9♭5 are also in common use, especially in jazz, and are constructed by altering the appropriate tones of the basic 9th chord.

Each major key contains a set of seven chords which are *diatonic* to that key. To say that a chord is diatonic to a key is to say that the chord is in that key and only contains notes from that key. Knowing the diatonic chords in any key is an important skill for any guitarist—it helps to know what chords are likely to show up in a given key.

Diatonic chords can be generated in the form of triads, 7th chords, 9th chords, 11th chords or 13th chords. Once you understand how to generate the triads, the same principles can be used for all of the other chord types.

Generating the Diatonic Triads of Any Key

1. Start with any major key (the example below is in C).

2. Stack 3rds above each scale degree. This forms a triad above each scale step. Use only notes found in that major key.

3. If you compare each resulting triad to a major scale with the same root, you will learn its quality (whether it is major, minor, etc.). For instance, compare the triad on D to the D Major scale, and you will see that this is a D Minor triad because it has ♭3 (F) instead of a 3 (3 is F♯ in a D Major scale). Number each chord with a Roman numeral. Use upper case for major triads, and lower case for minor and diminished triads. The resulting order of chord qualities will be:

Roman Numeral Review			
I or i	1	V or v	5
II or ii	2	VI or vi	6
III or iii	3	VII or vii	7
IV or iv	4		

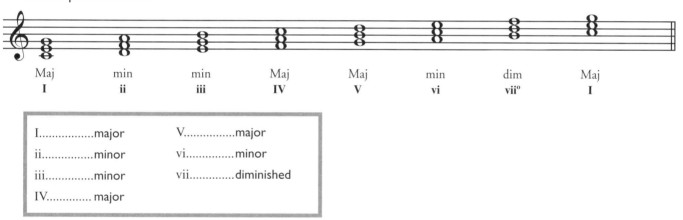

Maj	min	min	Maj	Maj	min	dim	Maj
I	**ii**	**iii**	**IV**	**V**	**vi**	**vii°**	**I**

I................major	V................major	
ii..............minor	vi..............minor	
iii..............minor	vii..............diminished	
IV..............major		

Diatonic 7th Chords

To form the diatonic 7th chords of any major key, stack another diatonic 3rd above the triads already generated. This produces the 7th of each chord. The resulting chord qualities are the following:

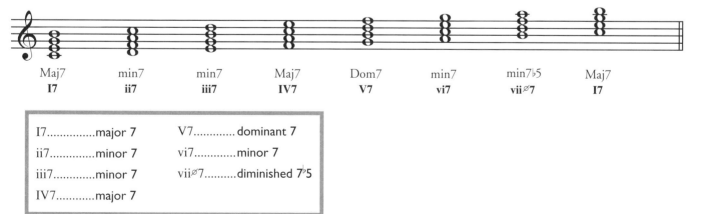

Maj7	min7	min7	Maj7	Dom7	min7	min7♭5	Maj7
I7	**ii7**	**iii7**	**IV7**	**V7**	**vi7**	**vii⌀7**	**I7**

I7..............major 7	V7..............dominant 7
ii7..............minor 7	vi7..............minor 7
iii7..............minor 7	vii⌀7..........diminished 7♭5
IV7..........major 7	

Tetrachords

Each major scale is composed of two intervalically identical halves called *tetrachords*. Each of these halves consists of this pattern: W–W–H.

This points out the fact that each major scale is a composite of two tetrachords taken from other major scales that border each other in the cycle of fifths.

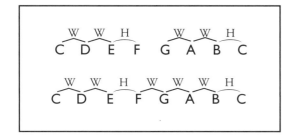

Observe how the second tetrachord in F is also the first tetrachord in C, and the second tetrachord in C is also the first tetrachord in G.

F Major	F G A B♭ C D E F				
C Major		C D E F G A B C			
G Major			G A B C D E F♯ G		
D Major				D E F♯ G A B C♯ D	
A Major					A B C♯ D E F♯ G♯ A

The above diagram illustrates exactly how each scale is composed of two tetrachords from its neighboring scales in the cycle of fifths. These neighboring scales are considered to be related because they are only one accidental removed from each other. Music can transition between related keys smoothly because so many notes are common to both keys. Understanding tetrachords will help you smoothly transition from one key to one of its related keys.

Inversions

To *invert* a chord is to rearrange its notes so that the 3rd, 5th or 7th is in the bass, instead of the root. On the guitar, many chords are played as inversions simply for the sake of convenience. The player may not even know he's using an inversion, because the notes all blend into the song he's playing. For example:

This D Major barre chord is in root position, with D in the bass:

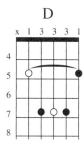

This D Major barre chord has A in the bass. It's easier to strum all of the strings, than to avoid the 6th string.

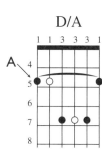

Below is the C Major triad in root position and all of its inversions.

Root Position	1 C	3 E	5 G	Root in Bass
1st Inversion	3 E	5 G	1 C	3rd in Bass
2nd Inversion	5 G	1 C	3 E	5th in Bass

PHOTO BY TIMOTHY RYAN PHELPS

Joe Satriani (b. 1956) is best known for his virtuoso playing on his solo albums (such as Surfing with the Alien *and* Flying in a Blue Dream*) and as founder of the G3 concert tours that have showcased guitar legends Steve Vai, Eric Johnson, Kenny Wayne Shepherd, Yngwie Malmsteen and others. He has toured with such diverse artists as Mick Jagger and Deep Purple. He is also a legendary guitar educator whose students include Steve Vai, Kirk Hammett, Larry LaLonde, David Bryson and Charlie Hunter.*

The inversions of a C Major 7th chord are the following:

Root Position	1 C	3 E	5 G	7 B		Root in Bass
1st Inversion	3 E	5 G	7 B	1 C		3rd in Bass
2nd Inversion	5 G	7 B	1 C	3 E		5th in Bass
3rd Inversion	7 B	1 C	3 E	5 G		7th in Bass

As long as the designated note is in the bass, the other notes can come in any order. Slash chord notation is used to label inversions. For example, if you look at the above chart, a 2nd inversion CMaj7 chord has a G in the bass, so it can be written as CMaj7/G.

The examples that follow illustrate how inversions can be used to enhance chord progressions. Notice how the use of the V chord in 1st inversion greatly improves the flow of example 151, as opposed to example 150.

Here is a I–V–vi chord progression in the key of C.

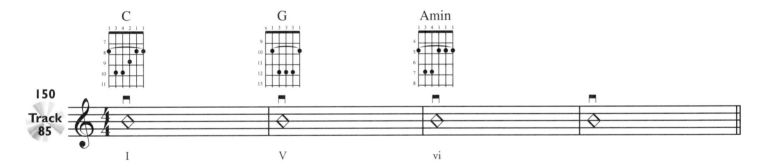

Here is the same progression from Example 150, but with a 1st inversion V chord.

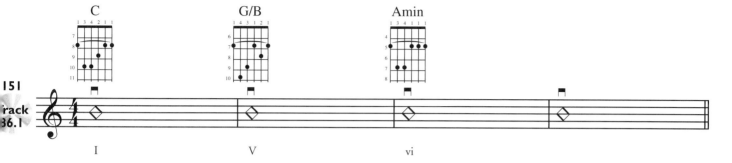

Here is a root position IV–I progression in the key of A Major.

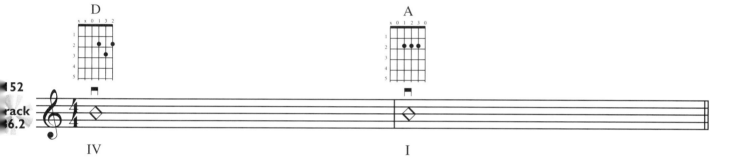

Here is the same progression from Example 152, but played with inversions. Notice the improved sound. Keith Richards of The Rolling Stones uses these inversions frequently.

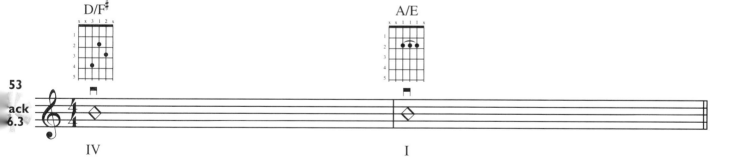

Minor Scales

The Natural Minor Scale

We learned earlier about the *natural minor scale*, which can also be called the Aeolian mode, and acts as the relative minor to a major key. The note names and intervals are shown below.

154
Track
87.1

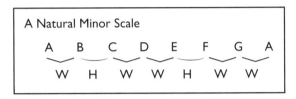

A Natural Minor Scale
A B C D E F G A
W H W W H W W

The Harmonic Minor Scale

The *harmonic minor scale* is very similar to the natural minor. In fact, it's exactly the same except that it has a ♮7. This scale has an "Arabian" sound, and is often used to create exotic modes (see page 56). The ♮7 creates an interval of 1½ steps between the 6th and 7th degrees of the scale, and this accounts for the exotic sound. The notes and intervals of the harmonic minor scale are shown below.

155
Track
87.2

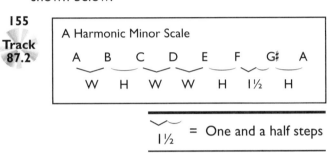

A Harmonic Minor Scale
A B C D E F G♯ A
W H W W H 1½ H

1½ = One and a half steps

The Melodic Minor Scale

The *melodic minor scale* differs from the harmonic minor scale in that it features the ♮6. This makes it just like a major scale, with a ♭3. This scale is often called "jazz minor," because its modes are used in jazz and fusion improvisation (see page 57). The note names and intervals of the melodic minor scale are shown below.

156
Track
87.3

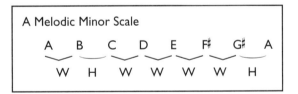

A Melodic Minor Scale
A B C D E F♯ G♯ A
W H W W W W H

Note: Several other sections in this book deal with theoretical topics that are closely related to this chapter. They are:

Slash Chords (page 21)
The Blues (page 25)
Chord Scales (page 48)
Exotic Scales (page 56)
Modes (page 74)

The Guitar Fretboard and Reading Diagrams

The Fretboard

This chart will help you find any note on the fretboard. Remember that the notes from frets 13 to 24 are the same as from frets 1 to 12, just one octave higher. Enharmonic equivalents are given wherever a note has two possible spellings (for example, A♯/B♭).

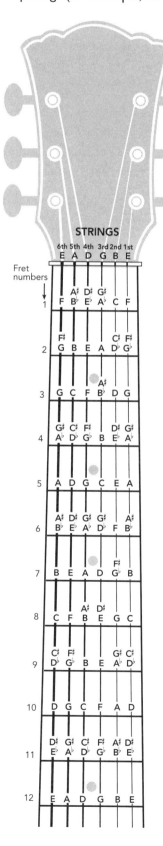

The Labeling of the Fingers

Left Hand
- (T) – Thumb
- (1) – Index
- (2) – Middle
- (3) – Ring
- (4) – Pinky

Right Hand
- (*p*) Pulgar – Thumb
- (*i*) Indice – Index
- (*m*) Medio – Middle
- (*a*) Anular – Ring
- (*c*) Chico – Pinky

Reading Chord Diagrams

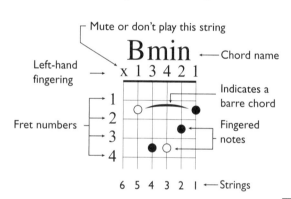

Scale Diagrams

The top line of a scale diagram represents the 1st (highest) string of the guitar, and the bottom line the 6th (lowest) string. The vertical lines represent frets which are numbered.

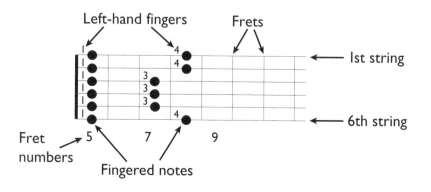

Reading Music

Standard Music Notation

Many guitarists learn how to play by listening, watching and just doing. Some of these players may be intimidated by the thought of reading, or feel that reading is unimportant because they've managed to get pretty good without it. What they don't realize is that reading music doesn't limit other ways of learning. It only adds to them. Reading helps a player get the most out of guitar textbooks and music lessons in general.

The Staff

The *staff* has five lines and four spaces which are read from left to right. At the beginning of the staff is a *clef*. The clef dictates which notes correspond to particular lines or spaces on the staff. Guitar music is written in *treble clef* 𝄞, which is sometimes called the *G clef*. The ending curl of the clef encircles the G line on the staff.

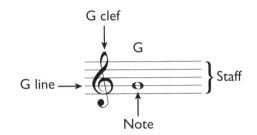

Most of the notes playable on the guitar are shown on the staff below. Notice that notes too high or too low to be written on the staff are given *ledger lines*.

Measures, Bar Lines and Time Signatures

The staff is divided by vertical lines called *bar lines*. The space between two bar lines is called a *measure*. Measures divide music into groups of *beats*. A beat is an equal division of time. Beats are the basic pulse behind music. A *double bar* marks the end of a section or example.

At the beginning of each piece of music is the *time signature*, which tells you how many beats are in a measure (the top number) and what rhythmic value (see Note Values below) receives one beat (the bottom number). In the case of $\frac{4}{4}$ time, there are four beats per measure and the quarter note (see Note Values below) received one beat.

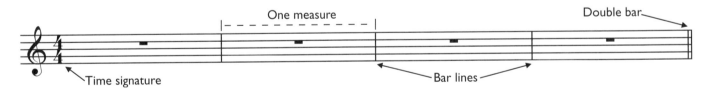

Note Values

As you know, the location of a note relative to the staff tells us its *pitch* (how high or how low it is). The duration, or *value*, is indicated by its shape. Here are the note values and their corresponding *rests*. A rest indicates silence.

This helpful chart shows the relationship between the note values.

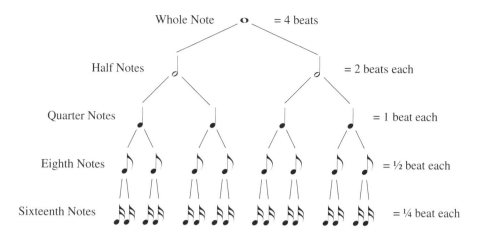

Ties

When notes are tied, the second note is not struck. Rather, its value is added to that of the first note. So, a half note tied to a quarter note would equal three beats.

Counting

Notice the numbers under the staff in these examples. They indicate how to count. Both of these examples are in time, so we count four beats in each measure. When there are eighth notes, which are only half a beat, we count "&" ("and") to show the division of the beats into two parts. When a counting number is in parentheses, a note is being held rather than struck.

Ties are a convenient way to notate notes that begin off the beat (on an "&").

Dots

A *dot* increases the length of a note by one half of its original value. For instance, a half note equals two beats. Half of its value is one beat (a quarter note). So, a *dotted half note* equals three beats (2 + 1 = 3). A dotted half note is equal to a half note tied to a quarter note.

Dotted notes are especially important when the time signature is $\frac{3}{4}$ time, because the longest note value that will fit in a measure is a dotted half note. Also, dotted notes are very important in $\frac{6}{8}$ time, because not only is a dotted half note the longest possible note value, but a dotted quarter note is exactly half of a measure (counted 1–2–3, **2**–2–3).

Tuplets

A *tuplet* is a rhythm that divides the beat differently than the standard multiples of two (eighth notes, sixteenth notes, thirty-second notes, and so forth). Tuplets are notated with a number above or below the notes that indicates how many parts the beat is divided into.

A *triplet* is a rhythm that divides the beat into three equal parts. Triplets are counted: 1–&–ah, 2–&–ah, 3–&–ah, 4–&–ah.

A *sextuplet* is a rhythm that divides the beat into six equal parts. It is twice as fast as a triplet in relation to the quarter note. It is counted: 1–2–3–4–5–6, 2–2–3–4–5–6, 3–2–3–4–5–6, 4–2–3–4–5–6.

A *quintuplet* is a rhythm that divides the beat into five equal parts. It is counted: 1–2–3–4–5, 2–2–3–4–5, 3–2–3–4–5, 4–2–3–4–5.

Rhythmic Notation

Rhythmic notation indicates rhythm but not pitch. This is often used to communicate strumming patterns for chords.

Reading Tablature

Tablature (TAB) is a means of notating the exact location of notes on the fretboard. The six lines correspond directly to the six strings of the guitar. The numbers on the lines indicate the frets that the left-hand fingers play. The numbers under the TAB staff tell you which left-hand fingers to use.

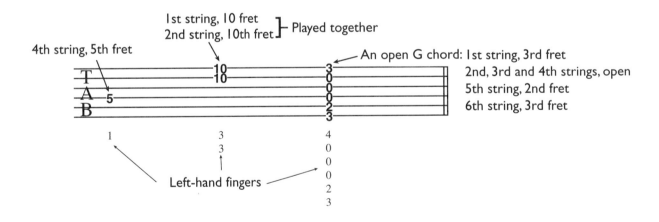

Final Note from the Author

Well, if you've made it this far, I suppose you have indeed "stayed on the neck!" Congratulations, that was a lot of work! Wasn't it?

Finishing a challenging book like this is not unlike getting a black belt in martial arts. It's a major achievement that one should be proud of. You now have the tools to become a master.

I'd like to stress the importance of experimentation and creativity. What an individual does with his skills determines whether he's just another guy who's self-absorbed, or maybe the next Jimi Hendrix. Music is a lifetime journey, one that defines and redefines our notions about personal limitations. If we try hard enough, we might surprise ourselves.

Listening to great music is key to mastering any musical style. I'd like to share some of my favorite rock guitar CDs, in no particular order. All of these have important lessons to teach and have inspired me greatly.

Steve Vai — *The 7th Song*

Yngwie Malmsteen — *Rising Force*

Joe Satriani — *Surfing With the Alien*

Stanley Clarke — *School Days*

Alex De Grassi — *The Water Garden*

Mattias IA Eklundh — *Freak Guitar: The Road Less Traveled*

Magic Elf — *Heavy Meddle; Elf Tales*

Di Meola/McLaughlin/De Lucia — *Friday Night in San Francisco*

Frank Zappa — *Overnight Sensation*

Pink Floyd — *The Wall; Wish You Were Here*

Van Halen — *Van Halen; Van Halen II*

Ozzy Osbourne — *Blizzard of Ozz*

Black Sabbath — *Heaven and Hell*

Michael Angelo Batio — *No Boundaries; Hands Without Shadows*

Jimi Hendrix — *Electric Ladyland; Are You Experienced?*

Judas Priest — *Painkiller*

Led Zeppelin — *IV (Zoso)*

Genesis — *Nursery Cryme*

King Crimson — *Discipline*

Stevie Ray Vaughan — *Couldn't Stand the Weather*

The Beatles — *Abbey Road*

Elizabeth Cotton — *Freight Train and Other North Carolina Folk Songs and Tunes*

Deep Purple — *Made In Japan*

Rage Against the Machine — *Rage Against the Machine*

Robert Johnson — *The Complete Recordings*

Enjoy, and good luck!

Sincerely,
Tobias Hurwitz